"Are you look_____ ...eet your two new best friends: Miriam and Laura. Pa_____ vague, useless advice, these two zero in on the specifics of how to make the right connections and what to say once you do. If you want to have a successful job search, begin with this book."

> **—Anita Bruzzese, *USA Today* columnist and author of**
> ***45 Things You Do That Drive Your Boss Crazy***

"It's all about how you communicate when it comes to landing your dream job, and if you've got even the slightest trouble in this area get *100 Conversations for Career Success*. From cold calling to leaving voice mail messages to nailing phone interviews, Laura Labovich and Miriam Salpeter have figured it out and offer their smart insights and advice. This book will seriously help you diminish those sweaty palm moments during your job hunt."

> **—Eve Tahmincioglu, career writer for Today.com and**
> **MSNBC.com, and CareerDiva.net blogger**

"*100 Conversations for Career Success* is a must-have for any job seeker. In the book, Miriam and Laura walk you through the most challenging part of the job search process—starting conversations with people you know (and don't know) who can help you find a job. I was particularly impressed with the level of detail they provide in scripts you can use to effectively communicate your message. Don't wait until you need this book to start reading it!"

> **—Sharlyn Lauby, SPHR, CPLP—president of ITM Group,**
> **Inc. and author of the blog *HR Bartender***

"With *100 Conversations*, Miriam and Laura have given job seekers what they've never had before—the ultimate resource for reaching out to contacts and potential new connections. With detailed examples and scripts, this invaluable guide will help jumpstart a new job search or revitalize an ongoing one. I highly recommend it."

> **—Liz Lynch, author, *Smart Networking: Attract a***
> ***Following In Person and Online***

"Far too many job-seekers are flummoxed by the questions, 'But what do I say?' and 'How do I say it?' when it comes to the conversations they need to be having to propel their job searches. They are often stymied to the point of stalling or derailing their searches. Now, here comes *100 Conversations for Career Success: Learn to Network, Cold Call, and Tweet Your Way to a Dream Job* as their salvation. Job hunters no longer need fumble for words as they learn to communicate effectively in situations ranging from networking, cold calling, informational interviewing, and through social media. This book will rescue many a job search."

—**Katharine Hansen, associate publisher/creative director, Quintessential Careers, www.quintcareers.com**

"This valuable new resource for job searchers breathes fresh life into the tried and true strategies of networking, cold calling, and informational interviews with real world guidance for what to say in almost every situation a job searcher might encounter in today's job market. And that's just the beginning—the latest strategies for bringing social media tools to the job search are a revelation. Again, Laura and Miriam do not disappoint—they provide detailed descriptions of everything you need to know about LinkedIn, Twitter, Facebook, and Google+ for maximum impact."

—**Dana Inerfeld, president, Catalyst Career Strategies**

"*100 Conversations* is the definitive answer to the #1 reason job seekers struggle in their job search—they lack a formula (or script) for what to say, when to say it, and how to say it to build their network, get the interview, and land the job. *100 Conversations* offers a solution and sample script for every situation a job seeker will face from voicemails and informational interviews to online social networking. No job seeker should be without it!"

—**Laura DeCarlo, president of the global career association, CareerDirectors International; author of *Interviewing: The Gold Standard* and *InterviewPocket RX*; co-author of JobSearch Bloopers**

"We all want to be more productive during job search, and, if we can, say the right things to the right people. *100 Conversations for Career Success* is a smart purchase for anyone out looking for a job. It not only tells you what to say in every imaginable situation, it will also lead to a more confident and purposeful use of your time."

   **—Tim Tyrell-Smith—founder, Tim's Strategy,**
      **http://timsstrategy.com**

"Building and maintaining solid connections are critical to creating opportunities in any field at any stage. Whether a recent graduate or experienced professional, if you want to connect authentically with others to further your job search, *100 Conversations* not only tells you how, but SHOWS you how. I plan on recommending it to my clients after they soul search and are ready to land their dream jobs!"

   **—Maggie Mistal, named one of the nation's best known**
      **career coaches by CNN, MaggieMistal.com**

"In this competitive market, it is vital to be able to ask for help during your transition. I have directly observed several thousand job seekers in the last three years; unfortunately, they're simply doing it wrong. The result? No one wants to or is willing to help them. There hasn't been a solution to this problem until now! Miriam and Laura put together a simple—yet powerful—book on how to get others on your side, and they have even given you all the recipes. All you have to do is follow their advice and guidelines and pretty soon you'll find yourself happily employed again. I highly recommend this book and give it two thumbs up!"

   **—Paul Anderson, career columnist and TV co-host,**
      **www.prolango.com**

"Miriam and Laura have taken the guesswork out your next job search. By thoughtfully contemplating virtually every scenario you may encounter, *100 Conversations* will instantly serve as your go-to resource for career success."

   **—Mark Stelzner, founder, Inflexion Advisors and**
      **JobAngels (now Hiring for Hope)**

"Bravo! Miriam and Laura have created a comprehensive step-by-step manual for job seekers. I finally have a resource I can point referrals, connections, friends, and colleagues to for all of their job-seeking advice. I spend hours each week discussing the variety of topics covered in *100 Conversations*—I will now be sharing this tool with all future candidates. This is the must-have manual for anyone looking for a job."

**—Heather McGough, staffing lead, Microsoft**
**Corporation, and 12-year Microsoft veteran**

"This engaging, practical book gives job seekers exactly the tips they need to handle every challenging job search situation—and there are many! From the crucial 20-second pitch to politely leveraging your network for job referrals, from cold calling to mentoring others, this book has it all, in a very accessible format. Highly recommended.

**—Heather Krasna, author, *Jobs That Matter: Find a Stable,***
***Fulfilling Career in Public Service* and Director of**
**Personal & Professional Development, Gabelli School,**
**Fordham University**

"Job searching often is not perceived as a friendly, engaging experience, and instead is seen as a lonely, frustrating and rejection-filled activity. Miriam and Laura's book truly helps disarm job seekers' apprehensions. I highly recommend *100 Conversations*, not only to job seekers, but to all careerists who want to take the helm of their career ship and sail into the sometimes tumultuous career waters with fearlessness and excitement."

**—Jacqui Barrett-Poindexter, partner and chief career**
**writer, CareerTrend, www.careertrend.net**

"This is must read for any job seeker! It's current, relevant, practical, and has real examples that can help job seekers at any level."

**—Seth L. Feit, regional vice president, Human Resources,**
**Time Warner Cable**

"No more excuses for not knowing what to say! Any question you've had about how to introduce yourself, what to say in letters and emails, how to write your profile bios, how to network online, and what to say on the phone; Miriam and Laura expertly address in this book so they easily and confidently roll off your tongue!"

—**Hannah Morgan, job search strategist,
www.careersherpa.net**

"My biggest screening criteria before I recommend a career book to clients (or dive into it myself) is whether or not it includes real, actionable advice. *100 Conversations for Career Success* does just that from cover to cover. I love the success stories and sample scripts and texts throughout as well as the boxed career success tips in every chapter. Two thumbs up and definitely earning a spot on my short list of recommended reading for clients!"

—**Laurie Berenson, CPRW, CEIC; Sterling Career
Concepts, LLC**

"Like a trusted coach sitting on your shoulder, this invaluable book will walk you through countless situations where you're wondering how to approach someone, how to present yourself, or how to properly follow up. Read it straight through the first time, but keep it on a low shelf as you'll be returning to it on a regular basis."

—**Marci Alboher, vice president, Encore.org and former
*New York Times* columnist**

"In today's world of multiple communication methods and ever-changing digital etiquette, *100 Conversations for Career Success* is a fantastic resource. I recommend it to any job seeker seeking expert tips, detailed scripts, and honest advice."

—**Lindsey Pollak, author, *Getting from College to Career:
Your Essential Guide to Succeeding in the Real World*,
www.lindseypollak.com**

"If you're looking for a new job or a making a career change, *100 Conversations for Career Success* is a must-read! This book is chock full of useful templates, amazingly helpful scripts, and general career tips—you won't believe how you survived without it. Miriam and Laura knocked it out of the park—and you're the beneficiary."

> —**Jodi Glickman, founder of Great on the Job (http://greatonthejob.com), author of *Great on the Job: What to Say, How to Say It, The Secrets of Getting Ahead*; contributor to *Harvard Business Review***

"This book is the job seeker's ultimate instruction manual. It is a practical, tactical guide to what you need to say and how to get your point across when contacting prospective recruiters and targeting employers to generate interviews. You don't ever need to be unsure about how to connect with hiring managers to get the results you want. Miriam and Laura provide multiple examples for almost all scenarios you will encounter to help you ultimately land your dream job."

> —**Lisa Rangel, managing director, Chameleon Resumes (http://chameleonresumes.com) and author of *The Do-It-Yourself Branded Resume Kit***

"What great advice! Laura and Miriam have given us a gift. Even the most inept networker, job seeker, and career novice will come out looking and acting like a pro if they follow even 10% of the suggestions in the book. I will be recommending this book to all my Career Development Facilitator certification students, and will pay close attention to these tips to move my own career forward."

> —**Janet E. Wall, EdD, CDFI, MCDP; president and founder, Sage Solutions and CEUonestop.com**

"While you've been networking since the first day you asked a new classmate for a toy in pre-K, knowing what to say and how to say it can get complicated—especially when you're exploring opportunities and trying to sell yourself for a new job at the same time. This quick start 'where you need it' guide, provides you with strategies and openers that will enable to you to go from tongue-tied to a master of effortless conversations—from cold calls and LinkedIn introductions to how to gently say no and recommend someone else when you're not the right person for the job. Read it. Study up. And go out and land your dream job."

—**Chandlee Bryan, co-author,** *The Twitter Job Search*
**Guide and career coach at BestFitForward.com**

"There's no single path to securing a job anymore. This book will help you learn how to present yourself better to employers so that you can get your dream job instead of settling."

—**Dan Schawbel, managing partner, Millennial Branding**
**and author of the international bestseller,** *Me 2.0*

# 100 CONVERSATIONS FOR CAREER SUCCESS

## LEARN TO NETWORK, COLD CALL, AND TWEET YOUR WAY TO YOUR DREAM JOB

LAURA M. LABOVICH
MIRIAM SALPETER

NEW YORK

Copyright © 2012 LearningExpress, LLC.

Published in the United States by LearningExpress, LLC, New York.

Library of Congress Cataloging-in-Publication Data:
Labovich, Laura M.
    100 conversations for career success : learn to network, cold call,
and tweet your way to your dream job / Laura M. Labovich and
Miriam Salpeter.
        p.   cm.
    Includes bibliographical references.
    ISBN-13: 978-1-57685-905-6 (alk. paper)
    ISBN-10: 1-57685-905-3 (alk. paper)
    1. Job hunting.   2. Job hunting—Computer network
resources.   3. Career development.   4. Online social networks.
    I. Salpeter, Miriam.   II. Title.   III. Title: One hundred
conversations for career success.
    HF5382.7.L33 2012
    650.14—dc23
                                                          2012010090


ISBN 978-1-57685-905-6

Printed in the United States of America.

9 8 7 6 5 4 3 2 1

For more information or to place an order, contact LearningExpress at:
    2 Rector Street
    26th Floor
    New York, NY 10006

# About the Authors

**Laura M. Labovich, MLRHR**, founder of The Career Strategy Group, is a job search makeover coach, in-demand speaker, and award-winning resume writer with more than a decade of experience in HR leadership at Fortune 100 companies including Walt Disney World and America Online, Inc.

Laura is known for saying she was "born and raised professionally at Disney," where she recruited nationwide for the highly competitive Walt Disney World College Program, led the recreation recruiting and staffing efforts for both Disney's Typhoon Lagoon and Disney's Blizzard Beach water parks, and was on the inaugural recruiting team for Disney's Animal Kingdom Theme Park.

At America Online, she developed and launched AOL's college internship program and coached hundreds of employees—from entry-level to executive—on how to fit in, stand out, and move up in the company and in their careers!

Laura partners with job seekers to develop effective targeted job search marketing plans that increase momentum and achieve breakthrough results. Laura inspires audiences with "profound results, a clear-minded vision, and personality all the way" and is known for offering both the "sizzle and the steak!" Laura's contagious enthusiasm and easy-to-implement approach has garnered

attention from major media outlets such as the *Washington Post,
U.S. News & World Report, USA Today*, and the *Chicago Tribune.*
Laura can be reached at lauramichelle@gmail.com or on the Web at
www.thecareerstrategygroup.com. She lives in Bethesda, Maryland,
with her husband and two children.

**Miriam Salpeter, MA**, is a sought-after job search and social networking coach, author, and speaker. Featured on CNN and quoted
by major media outlets, including the *Wall Street Journal*, the *New
York Times*, Forbes.com, and others, she is owner of Keppie Careers,
a coaching and consulting firm.

Readers called Miriam's first book, *Social Networking for Career
Success*, "a masterpiece in social media and personal branding" and
named it "destined to become a bible for savvy careerists." Highly
regarded by top experts, Miriam is on CNN's list of "top 10 job
tweeters you should be following." Monster.com included her in
their "11 for 2011—Career Experts Who Can Help Your Job Search"
and respected online resource, Quintessential Careers, called her a
"Top 15 Career Mastermind." In addition to her own blog, Miriam
writes for *U.S. News & World Report*'s On Careers column and is a
contributing writer for AOL Jobs and Salary.com.

Miriam helps job seekers and entrepreneurs leverage social media
and traditional tools to achieve their goals. She offers clients clarity,
confidence, and know-how. Miriam transforms resumes, creates
professionally branded online profiles, and teaches job seekers and
business owners how to compete in a fast-paced market.

A vice president for a Wall Street firm prior to earning a master's
degree from Columbia University, Miriam headed the Career Action
Center at the Rollins School of Public Health of Emory University
before launching her business. She lives in Atlanta with her husband
and three boys.

The best ways to reach Miriam are via her website:
www.keppiecareers.com or on Twitter @Keppie_Careers.

# Acknowledgments

To our talented colleagues: thank you for generously sharing your time, expertise, and scripts. We are especially grateful to the incredible members of Career Directors International (CDI): thank you for your contributions, support, and friendship. We are indebted to our clients: thank you for sharing your struggles about what to say when in a job search. You inspired us to write this book. It was wonderful working with the LearningExpress team, especially editor (and fearless leader) Sheryl Posnick, who championed our ideas and gave us the opportunity to bring this book to fruition.

**From Laura:**
To my loving, supportive, and treasured parents: I have created a life I love because of your support and encouragement. Thank you, thank you for always being my soft place to fall.

Thank you to my wonderful husband, Matt, for believing I would one day write a book, and for making me believe it, too. I could not have done this without you.

To my beautiful children: thank you for lighting up my life. I feel so very blessed to have a career that allows me to greet your smiling faces at the bus stop every day.

To the dedicated members of my Career Cafe of Bethesda: thank you for your willingness to share your job-search trials and tribulations, and for creating an incredible, collaborative community.

And, lastly, to Miriam, for pushing me when I could no longer push myself, for giggling with me (when we really should have been working!), and for sharing this journey with me. You are more than a co-author to me; you are a dear and trusted friend.

**From Miriam:**

I am so fortunate to have an amazing husband whose love and support make it possible for me to pursue my goals. Thank you, Mike, for everything you do to keep our family afloat.

Thanks to my wonderful sons for inspiring me to do my very best every day so I can try to set a good example—and for being quiet when I am working!

I appreciate my friends and colleagues, including those I've met in person and the community of people I only know via social-media exchanges. My work and life are so much richer because of what I learn from you every day.

Laura—I am so glad you shared your idea for this book and grateful we've had this chance to work together. We've had spirited debates over words, phrases, and sentences in an effort to say everything exactly the right way, but always with good humor and mutual respect. I'm fortunate to have you as a trusted colleague and good friend.

I am dedicating this book in memory of my dad, Michael P. Cohen. Throughout his life and career as a social worker, he demonstrated a high level of integrity, compassion, and commitment to helping people meet their potential. I hope to do the same.

# Contents▶

# CONTENTS

Additional resources for career success are included on our website: **100conversationsforcareersuccess.com**.

Related title: *Social Networking for Career Success*, Miriam Salpeter.

# Scripts by ▶ Chapter

# SCRIPTS BY CHAPTER

# Foreword

Landing a job, whether it's in a good economy or a tough economy, can be a difficult and stressful experience. However, access to advice from those who have been through it before—those really in the know—can help you better navigate through the storm. The information in *100 Conversations for Career Success* is invaluable for job seekers who want a guide to help steer them successfully.

Conversations, like those outlined in this book, and both in-person and online social connections, can help you achieve greater professional success and job satisfaction; I've seen myself at Glassdoor how important it is to have access to useful information to help job seekers get a foot in the door.

Through the powerful words and important conversations in this book, I'm confident you'll be armed and ready to tackle any challenge in your career, from casual networking interactions to important engagements with VIPs. You will be able to use the examples in this book to help accomplish any job search goal.

I wish you the best along all stages of your career path and encourage you to always engage in conversations, using the tips and advice outlined in this book, to not just find a job, but to land the job you've only dreamed of.

> **—Robert Hohman, CEO & co-founder of Glassdoor,
> www.glassdoor.com, a leading social jobs and career
> community**

# Introduction

We could have called this book *What to Say and How to Say It in Your Job Search* because in it we teach you to comfortably and successfully communicate, online and off-line, to land a job faster. Within these pages, you will find scripts to help you clarify and pitch what you offer, access and impress VIPs, and make a great impression in person, on the phone, and via social media tools such as LinkedIn, Twitter, Facebook, and Google+.

This book will arm you with tools to overcome job-search jitters and inspire you to confidently reach out to contacts you would not otherwise approach. Use it as your guide and the scripts, templates, outlines, and real-life examples as starting points to help you create meaningful and compelling interactions. You are unique, and your materials should reflect what is special about you, so use these as a blueprint and customize your communications to reflect what you offer.

When you are done, we hope you'll say without hesitation, "I CAN DO THIS!"

# Introducing Yourself: How to Communicate What You Offer

**CHAPTER**

## Your Elevator Pitch

**Y**ou know you have a lot to offer an employer. Yet when you need to talk about yourself, you're tongue-tied! Maybe it's ironic, but the thing we've been doing all our lives—introducing ourselves—can be anxiety-producing during a job search. "Hello, my name is" isn't going to cut it. You need to learn how to reel in your listeners and convince them they need to learn more about you. Imagine you only have a short elevator ride to impress someone. Are you ready to push the "up" button and get started, or are you running for the stairs?

The trick? Don't overdo it. You may have heard about the "two-minute elevator speech," and while pitches of this length do have their place (for example, at formal networking events or interview settings), in most cases, shorter sound bites sell. Put yourself in the other person's shoes—when you're meeting someone for the first time, are you really going to listen to his entire two-minute introduction? Or, at about 20 or 30 seconds in, will your mind wander to that night's dinner plans? In this chapter, we're going to show you how to prioritize key details to help win your listener's attention.

You should include the following topics when you compose your pitch:

- What is your goal/objective?
- What do you want to do? (Consider your audience's needs.)
- What impact do you have?
- What results do you create?
- What problem(s) do you solve?
- How do you create positive results?

### ⇨ TIP

If you are speaking to an audience unfamiliar with your industry, be sure your pitch is free of industry-specific jargon, terms, and abbreviations. Try to speak in sound bites, as if members of the media will be quoting you.

Do your research to help identify what skills, experiences, and accomplishments your target employers appreciate.

- Comb through job descriptions.
- Review information outlined in your professional association's materials.
- Keep an eye on what thought leaders in your field are sharing via social media outlets (including blogs, LinkedIn, Twitter, and Google+).
- Talk to people about industry trends.

Here is a template to keep in mind when you write your pitch. You can adjust the order once you decide what to include:

*I work with* [target audience] *to* [what problem you solve]. *This is how* [your impact/results].

# Before and After Pitches

Consider this "before" pitch:

*I have been a project manager and consultant for various companies within the D.C. area* [this is a little vague], *and I am mainly interested in energy and sustainability, climate change, and environmental readiness. I last worked for Company X doing green I.T. and helping with environmental issues. I'm looking for a job where I can have an impact on green initiatives* [no "problem I solve" or impact/results].

How can the speaker better organize this to help the audience understand his value?

Consider this revised pitch:

**One sentence:** *I'm an award-winning expert in green project management, and I have saved my company more than $65,000 per year.*

Once you perfect a short version of your pitch, build on it to create various ways to introduce yourself in more formal settings.

**Short pitch:** *As a project manager and senior adviser in the environmental energy industry* [target audience], *I've had a significant impact on energy and environmental policies and can bridge the gap between the technical community and management interests* [problem I solve]. *At Company X, I developed and led a green-I.T. project that resulted in a 30% reduction in electricity costs—translating to a savings of $65,000 per year* [my impact/results].

**Longer pitch:** *As a project manager and senior adviser in the environmental energy industry* [target audience] *for the past 15 years, I've had a significant impact on energy and environmental policies. I'm unique among engineers. I can bridge the gap between the technical community and management interests* [problem I solve]. *At Company X, I developed and led a green-I.T. project that resulted in a 30% reduction in electricity costs—translating to a savings of $65,000 per year. The project won a technical-excellence award, and I, along with others on the effort, won individual achievement awards* [my impact/results].

# More Short, Impactful Pitches

How can you explain what you offer in as few words as possible so that you don't lose the person's attention? Even if your pitch is short, you can still include your most important information. Review these short examples as you begin to craft a sound bite about your accomplishments:

*As a sales trainer and coach for medium-sized businesses* [target audience], *I analyze and identify sales organizations' shortcomings and use my technological and facilitation experience to create efficient, effective, and profitable sales organizations* [problem I solve]. *My last client showed a 50% increase in callbacks after only one training* [my impact/results].

*As an attorney with experience investigating fraud, waste, and abuse in government programs* [target audience], *I examine fund applications, contracts, bidding documents, reports, and invoices to make sure my department doesn't waste any resources* [problem I solve]. *As a result of my efforts, we saved over $1.5 million during the last year alone* [my impact/results].

## SHORT, IMPACTFUL PITCHES

Meg Guiseppi, founder of Executive Career Brand, a branding and resume-writing company for CEOs and high-level executives, offers the following short pitches that would be most intriguing to an audience. Who wouldn't want to learn more about you once you powerfully articulate what you offer? For example:

*I'm a turnaround management expert in the federal sector. I take on challenges no one would touch and transform losers into profitable organizations.*

*I'm a start-up CEO and business-development leader in high tech. I convince Fortune 500 companies to risk multi-million dollar commitments on the new, untried products of emerging enterprises.*

continued from page 4

> *I'm a fearless change agent in manufacturing revitalization. I envision and execute game-changing turnarounds FAST, get returns NOW, and bullet-proof companies against today's highly volatile global marketplace.*

# CREATE STEP-UP PITCHES FOR DIFFERENT AUDIENCES

Barbara Safani, owner of Career Solvers, a resume-writing and job-search consultancy, created this "build-on" pitch series, which starts with a very short blurb and ends with more in-depth descriptions. Think about how you use these various pitches when you introduce yourself, keeping in mind that the more involved versions may be most appropriate during formal interview settings. Once you know what problems people in your field are trying to solve, you'll be able to gear your pitch to their needs.

## Twenty-Second Version #1

> *I identify a company's pain points and business goals as they relate to the brand value proposition and the customer experience and then bridge the gap between where they are now and where they want to be.*

## Long Version #1

> *I am a business-strategy innovator with extensive experience creating road maps that build a company's brand value proposition. I identify product expansion opportunities and promote customer loyalty. I uncover a company's pain points and business goals and then bridge the gap between where they are now and where they want to be. I am successful in this role for the following three reasons:*
>
> - *For Company A, I boosted online applications for the business credit card by 60% by recognizing the need to shift emphasis away from the saturated consumer-card market and toward the more lucrative small business segment.*
> - *For Company B, I extended the brand in the B2B space by creating a product-optimization strategy and identifying new verticals for the company's innovative custom-fit apparel software application.*

5

continued from page 5

- *For Company C, I increased gross margins by close to 30% by transforming this low-margin photographic supplies discounter into an early adopter of digital photography solutions and a lucrative reseller of digital imaging supplies and equipment.*

## Twenty-Second Version #2

*I align various siloed lines of businesses to build consensus, better communicate a brand's value proposition, and improve the customer experience.*

## Long Version #2

*I align various siloed lines of businesses to build consensus, better communicate a brand's value proposition, and improve the customer experience. I am successful in this role for the following reasons:*

- *For Company A, I created a strategic road map for an enterprise-wide initiative to streamline 398 web properties across nine countries, resulting in exceptional ease of navigation, improved user experience, and more consistent brand messaging.*
- *For Company B, I helped companies crystallize their brand value proposition and business goals by aligning stakeholders and project teams, and building more systematized and integrated development processes to work through business complexities and deliver a superlative customer experience.*

## Twenty-Second Version #3

*I mobilize and motivate teams through periods of change and growth.*

## Long Version #3

*I mobilize and motivate teams through periods of change and growth:*

- *At Company A, I turned around the performance of a floundering customer-experience team while cutting costs by 35% and renewing client confidence.*
- *At Company B, I managed the development of websites and built teams and infrastructures from scratch. In both cases I*

continued from page 6

*sourced top talent, streamlined costs, and systematized work-flow to improve the operation.*

*In addition, earlier in my career I was a digital artist, photographer, videographer, producer, and creative director, and I was also an adjunct professor at the School of Visual Arts, The New School, and New York City Technical College, CUNY, where I taught Ideas in Computer Art, Concept Development, and TV Advertising Design and Production courses. I have an MFA in photography, video, multi-media, and digital imaging, and an MS in social psychology and organizational behavior and management. I hold a certification in e-commerce and e-customer relationship management, and I was certified by Scient to facilitate innovation training.*

*My professional aspirations at this time are to partner with a forward-thinking organization to align the company or client's brand value proposition with achievable business goals, serve as the customer advocate, innovate, create best practices, and ensure a superior return on investment to shareholders*

# How to Create Your Pitch

### About You

What skills and accomplishments set you apart from every other person in the room? In your industry?

### About Your Industry

What skills do you see over and over again in your target job descriptions? (List 5–10.)

What problems are speakers at your professional conferences addressing? (List 3–5.)

Who are the thought leaders in your field, and what are they saying? (List 3–5 people who create regular content via blogs or other social media tools. Make a point to connect with them and to read your favorites.)

### What You Do

What is your goal/objective (including your target audience)?

What do you want to do? How does it relate to what your audience wants?

What problem(s) do you solve?

What results do you create?

---

**CAREER SUCCESS STEPS**

**Remember this format:**

*I work with* [target audience] *to* [what problem you solve]. *This is how* [your impact/results].

---

# 2

# How to Wow Your Audience on the Phone

In the age of texting and tweeting, employers still reach for the phone when they want to talk to you. While dropped calls and background noise have become the norm, don't overlook telephone etiquette. It's true: your outgoing voicemail message could be stunting your job search potential. (Ironic disclaimer: We know none of the following applies to "you," but take a look anyway, in case your "friend" can benefit from it!)

## What Phone Number Do You Provide?

It sounds obvious, but when you list a phone number on your resume or application materials, assume an employer will eventually use it to contact you. Think about who is answering your phone, what answering message the employer may hear, and what he or she will think of you. It's probably a good idea to list a number no one but you would ever answer (probably a mobile number), and then be mindful that an employer may be calling any time you answer your phone.

## Your Outgoing Message

Take the time to evaluate your outgoing phone greeting.

- Does it contain music?
- Can you hear a child's voice?
- Is there background noise?
- Does it make an effort at humor? Is it "cute"?
- Is it political? Religious?

If you answered yes to any of these questions, stop everything you are doing and change your message now! Record a simple greeting:

*Hello, you have reached April Showers. Please leave your name, number, and a short message, and I will return your call as soon as possible. Thank you.*

You may choose to include a mini-pitch in your outgoing message. Only do this if it will appeal to all potential employers (don't worry about what friends and family think):

*Hello. This is Sam Browning, human-resources and training expert. I'm sorry I can't take your call now. Please leave your name and number, and I'll get back to you as soon as possible.*

Another suggestion is to provide an email address as an option for callers:

*Hello, this is search engine optimization expert Raymond Smith. Please leave a message, or feel free to contact me via email at Raymond dot Smith at Gmail dot com. I'll get back to you as soon as I can.*

Listen to your greeting. Is it garbled? Did you rush it, as if you were escaping a fire but wanted to record the message first? Try again! Ask your hard-of-hearing neighbor to call and listen. Does he understand what you said? If so, you are golden.

## Be Conscious of When You Answer Your Phone

Providing a mobile phone number may avoid a sticky and embarrassing situation. When you provide a number that only you answer, your kids won't be tempted to tell a potential employer you are stuck up a tree trying to rescue the cat, or "in the bathroom and won't be out for a LONG time." However, only you can make sure you don't answer the phone under inconvenient circumstances.

Once your resume is out there, be aware that *any time* the phone rings, it might be your dream job on the line. Years ago, when Miriam was working on Wall Street (and mobile phones were a lot less common), she called a candidate for a job. The candidate answered her cell phone—from a loud, New York City street corner. You can imagine the conversation:

> **Miriam:** We'd like to see about scheduling an interview . . .
>
> **Candidate:** I'm sorry . . . I can't really hear you so well. It's really LOUD here. Let me try to get somewhere quieter.
>
> **Miriam:** Okay. [Waiting . . . thinking, *Why did she answer the phone if she can't hear me?*]
>
> **Candidate:** Okay—I think this is better . . .
>
> **Miriam:** We'd like to have you come in for an interview. When is a good time?
>
> **Candidate:** Oh, this isn't any better. Can I call you back?
>
> **Miriam:** [Thinking, *It hardly matters what I say—she can't hear me.*] Okay. Bye.

While it was great to be able to reach this candidate (in theory) when she was out and about—a communication revolution at the time—in reality, she would have been better off allowing voice-mail to pick up and returning the call when she was in a quieter place.

That was more than 15 years ago. Unfortunately, it doesn't seem as if we've learned much about telephone etiquette in the interim; it isn't uncommon for us to answer our phones whenever they ring, out of habit or fear of missing something important.

If you're in a bad or loud spot, let the call go to voicemail (to your nice, clear, professional greeting!). Listen to the message and call back as soon as possible. You don't want to be screaming, "So sorry, I can't HEAR you," or cursing the driver who just cut you off as you were answering your phone. Neither offers the impression you want to give your prospective employer.

## Answering the Phone

Assuming you're in a quiet place with no distractions and have access to a pen and paper in case you need to take notes, think about how you answer your phone. Most often, our default greeting is simply "hello." Consider making it easier for the caller:

*Hello, this is Jim Roy.*
*Good morning, Jim Roy here.*

Danielle Powers, founder of Power in Recruiting, a training firm, reminds readers that recruiters often phone candidates to screen them before deciding whether to invite them for an interview. She suggests keeping the following tips in mind to be well prepared for a recruiter's call:

## Danielle's Do's

- Smile! The caller can hear it in your voice.
- Be in a quiet area free from distractions. If you are not, ask if you can call back in short order, meaning 10 to 15 minutes, if possible.
- Leave a copy of your resume in a folder in your car. If you are out shopping or out to eat, your car is your office.
- Ask a great open-ended question. For example:

*I did want to mention, not all of my skills and expertise are detailed on my resume. It is accurate; however, it is hard to put my entire career onto one page. Are there specific focus areas or experiences* [name something you are proficient in, for example, working with C-level managers or designing a specific type of window or a specific technology or software] *this job requires?*

- Talk about lessons learned and opportunities achieved specific to you and your expertise.
- Give examples in response to questions regarding your performance and success. Write down three strong quantitative success stories as bullet points and have them printed out in a folder next to your computer and in your car, for example:

    *As an executive assistant, I created an electronic filing process for our office. It not only made me and the other office assistants more effective, but it also saved the company money on storage for our files.*

or

    *As a manufacturing technician, I was working on a new product line. There was one area where the plastic kept catching and causing a backup in production. I worked with the engineer to troubleshoot the spot. It saved us from*

*throwing away tens of thousands of pieces and spending a
lot of man hours in rework.*

or

*As a customer-service professional, I was assisting one of
our smaller customers. Through my close relationship with
my contact, I discovered they were using a competitor for a
service we offered; she did not even realize we provided that
service! I explained our options and connected her with our
salesperson. We ended up increasing sales from that company from $2,000 a year to $22,000.*

- If the recruiter does not want to pursue an interview, ask,
  "What is missing in my background or career goals for this
  particular opportunity?"

## Danielle's Don'ts

- Don't be put off by not having all of the information about
  the job up front.
- Don't ramble on and on about your old employer. It's never
  a good idea to badmouth an employer, but even if you have
  positive things to say, avoid making the conversation about a
  previous company or boss.
- Don't push for more details about the job before you answer
  questions about your resume. This is not a give-and-take call
  where they ask a question and you ask one back.
- Don't be too formal or too personal; be yourself, but don't
  try to make friends. For example, don't say:
  - *When are you looking to hire someone? I would have to
    make daycare arrangements.*
  - *What do you enjoy best about your job?*
  - *What are the benefits? My family really needs them.*
  - *I don't have all the experience you are looking for, so I am not
    sure if you think I am a good candidate. Do the other people
    you are talking to have everything you are looking for?*

These are topics to save for a second interview. Instead, say something along these lines:

- *Based on the information you have shared and the enthusiasm that you have for the company, it sounds like a wonderful opportunity and very much like the type of organization I have been looking for. I am eager to move toward a next step.*
- *Is there anything I can review in regard to the job or company prior to a next step that would provide me with additional information about your organization?*
- *I know that you mentioned in this position you need to be an expert at Excel. I would rate myself as more beginner to intermediate. I know the community college offers weeklong classes that would get me up to speed. I will check this evening to see when the next one is. I have been meaning to do that.*

Follow these tips to leave a more positive impression and set yourself up for what follows—getting the word out about your job search.

## Career Success Steps

Even small details such as your outgoing voicemail message matter and can affect the outcome of your job search. Once you can articulate your value and handle yourself well on the phone, you will be on your way to landing a new job.

- Listen to your telephone answering machine greeting. Make sure it is completely professional and includes only your voice.
- Write down three strong quantitative success stories as bullet points.
- Print your list and your resume to keep in a folder near your computer and in your car.

# How to Inform Your Network You're Searching for a Job

Once you create your elevator pitch and prepare a great outgoing voice message, you are ready to tell your network—family, friends, neighbors, former colleagues—that you are looking for work and ask for their support.

In this stage, your goal is to gain buy-in from your friends and colleagues by offering them enough information so they can be your allies. But a quick word of caution before you communicate to your network—don't approach your closest contacts with a metaphorical *J* (for job seeker) on your forehead. This turns every conversation into a game of "Who do YOU know who can help me?" If your contacts perceive you as needy, they will avoid you. Instead, remember that you are a job seeker only temporarily; you have lots of other wonderful gifts, skills, and talents to offer, and you do not need to make your job search the only topic of conversation. Your friends will want to help, we promise!

# Your Email Address

Before you launch into communicating verbally with your network, make sure you secure a professional email address. No one will take you seriously if you use a silly or inappropriate email. For example, replace amyover50@hotmail.com (yes, a real job seeker's address) or hotmama72@aol.com with an email using some variant of your name *only*. You may also consider either a Gmail address or an address with your own domain, for example, john@johnsmith.com. Either choice helps you appear up-to-date with technology.

# Email Blasts

### *What Not to Do: Sample Email*

Recently laid off, Joseph began his job search with a mass email to 75 of his closest friends, former colleagues, and neighbors, asking for their help with his campaign. Here's what he wrote:

Hello Friends and Family,

I am continuing my job hunt and would love your help. I hope this isn't too much to ask. If you can, please think of me if there are any openings at your company or any other openings you hear of. If you do know of anything, please pass along my information. I have attached my resume and my LinkedIn profile is also below. I would be interested in a variety of positions, including, but not limited to:

- Sales Representative
- Account Manager
- Corporate Trainer
- Recruiter
- Supply Chain Management
- Tutor
- Office Manager or Receptionist
- Consultant
- Sales Support

Please let me know if you hear of anything. I appreciate any help you can give!

Thanks!
Joseph

Not surprisingly, his approach did not yield any results.

How did such a well-intentioned email go so wrong? First, he asked his network to think of him when and if ". . . there are any openings at your company that you hear of."

Even in a retrenching economy, we still pass by the local grocery store plastered with "Now Hiring" signs. By asking his friends and family to keep an eye out for openings, he missed the boat because his request was *not specific enough.*

As the email wore on, we speculate he became a bit more anxious and did not want to limit himself, so he said:

"I would be interested in a variety of positions, including, but not limited to," and then offered a laundry list of dissimilar positions. By positioning himself as a jack-of-all-trades, he confused the audience. Having a lack of focus positioned him as a master of none.

Joseph had the right idea—to reach out to his network to seek help. The problem was in his approach; he missed an opportunity to engage his colleagues, friends, neighbors, and acquaintances with information they could really use. It is likely his contacts had inroads at companies where he might like to work, but without his targeted guidance, they were unable to help. Instead, spoon-feed it to them. Write a comprehensive Personal Marketing Plan (PMP) spelling out exactly where you want to work, what you want to do, and why. In fact, make it so clear what you do and what you need that your friends will be able to accurately describe your job targets in just one sentence.

## What Is a PMP?

The purpose of a Personal Marketing Plan (PMP) is to facilitate productive conversations with others who can assist in your quest for a job. A PMP is often referred to as a road map for your career or a mission statement for your job search. Regardless of title, its single function is to stimulate meaningful dialogue to give your job search forward momentum. See a sample PMP on the next page.

# EXHIBIT 1: SAMPLE PERSONAL MARKETING PLAN FOR KEVIN HART

**Target Functions:**

Vice President / Director of Environmental, Safety, and Health

**Strengths:**

- Strong business partner; able to link ES&H direction with company strategy. Extensive record of executing ES&H in global and developing markets.
- Lead positive and sustained organizational change. Executive leader, culture builder, and program developer for large and Fortune 1000 companies. Adept in managing across matrixed and decentralized organizations.
- Well versed in effective negotiations with regulatory bodies on the national and international landscape.
- Demonstrated abilities to analyze process and systematic deficiencies. Proven success controlling costs while governing budgets of $20+ million, over 100 reports in 30 countries.
- Customer-centric focus.

**Company Attributes:**

- Values sustainability and diversity and views ES&H as a company value.
- Understands the link between safety, quality, and other business drivers.
- Views ES&H as a company value.
- Committed to making a positive impact on its employees and communities.
- Realizes that management controls most of the ingredients of a safe working environment.

**Location:  Detroit, MI, and Cleveland, OH**

**Target Companies and Industries:**

| **Aerospace and Defense** | **Utilities, Gas & Electric** | **Food & Consumer Products** |
|---|---|---|
| Boeing | Exelon | PepsiCo |
| United Technologies | Southern Company | Kraft Foods |
| Northrop Gruman | FPL Group | General Mills |
| General Dynamics | Dominion Resources | ConAgra Foods |
| Honeywell International | Consolidated Edison | Sara Lee |
| Raytheon | Duke Energy | Kellogg |
| Textron | Xcel Energy | H.J. Heinz |
| Goodrich Corporation | Scana | Coca-Cola Company |
|  | Constellation Energy | Coca-Cola Enterprises |
| **Petroleum Refining/ Production** |  | Procter & Gamble |
|  | **Manufacturing** | Colgate Palmolive |
| Exxon Mobil | Michelin | United Parcel Service |
| Chevron | BMW North America | Home Depot |
| Conoco Phillips | Altria Group | FedEx Corporation |
| Valero Energy | Ford Motors | Nike |
| Marathon Oil | Kodak | Lowes |
| Hess | Hewlett Packard | General Mills |
| Occidental Petroleum | General Motors | SC Johnson |
| Apache | Chrysler |  |
| Chesapeake Energy | Toyota North America |  |
| BP |  |  |
| Nucor |  |  |

The typical components of a PMP include:

- Target jobs
- Industry or company size
- Geographic region
- A list of companies you are targeting
- Company attributes
- Your strengths or preferred responsibilities

Many job seekers are concerned that by being specific and sharing titles (PR manager/director), companies (Discovery Communications/Disney), and geographic regions (D.C.-metro area only), they might miss an opportunity, say, at a junior level, or in a neighboring state not on the list. But, in fact, it is just the opposite! A narrow job target will enable your network to reach out to the right companies, in the right locations; if your list is too broad, then your request will fall on deaf ears.

## ⇨ CAREER SUCCESS TIP

De-bulk your mass emails. Send personal emails to your acquaintances and neighbors. Call your friends, one by one, and then follow up with emails outlining your specifics.

Broadcasting to a gazillion people and asking for jobs within multiple functions is not a good strategy. Remain focused, determine your one to three job targets (titles) and companies, and create a pitch for each of them. Then share these with your network.

### Sample Email to Close Friends and/or Neighbors

Dear Susan,

As you may know, Company Q had its third round of layoffs last week, and I was affected. It was a rough week, but I am really looking forward to finding my next great job. You have always been such a great support for me in offering your help, so I hope you won't mind my request.

I have thought about the types of companies that "wow" me and where I believe I can make a huge impact, and I've made a list below.

I'm looking for a position in Environmental Health and Safety at the Director level or above, so if you know of anyone at the following companies, I would genuinely welcome an introduction. As you know, I'm looking to stay in the Washington, D.C., area.
Target companies include: [Company A, B, C, D, E, F, G].

End on a personal note:

I'll see you at the neighborhood Halloween party in a few weeks! Looking forward to catching up!

In this message, the job seeker lists target companies, field, and job title, along with his level (manager), location preference, and the level of the people he'd like to meet.

## Sample In-Person Conversation with Friends

What if you encounter someone in a more informal setting, for example, a community barbeque or block party? As you bite into a juicy hot dog, your neighbor asks how your job search is going. Typically, here's what most job seekers say:

> **You:** *It's going well, I suppose. Hey, now that you mention it, I've been meaning to ask if you would consider taking my resume to the head of marketing at your company.*

You may get an offer such as this one (job seekers hear *this* all the time):

> **Neighbor:** *I'd be happy to take your resume and circulate it around.*

These moments offer terrific potential when you make an effort to keep control of the situation and lay out your strategy in advance. Remember, most people have contacts with folks beyond their own companies. Have a few of your target companies memorized, so they will roll off your tongue:

**Neighbor:** *I'd be happy to take your resume and circulate it around.*

**You:** *I sure appreciate that. You know, recently I made a list of some companies where I'd like to meet some people. Can I share some of those names with you?*

**Neighbor:** *Sure, I'd be happy to help.*

**You:** *Thanks so much!* [Name companies.] *Would you be able to make any introductions? There's nothing open at my level at these companies right now. That's why I'd like to speak with them before they open a position, to learn about the organizations and see if working there would be a fit.*

**Neighbor:** *I do know someone at* [one of your target companies]. *I'd be happy to take your resume to him.*

Don't fall victim to the resume drop and run! If you give your resume away, you'll lose control of the situation. You won't get a contact number, and you won't be able to follow up. Your resume could end up in the garbage can and you'll never know it. Don't give up—push harder.

**You:** *Thank you! Could you give me his name and contact info so I can follow up after he's received my resume?*

**Neighbor:** *I'll get you his contact info today.*

## Sample Script for Reaching Out to Long-Lost Friends and Colleagues

At some point in your job search, you may need to reach out to a former colleague or friend you haven't seen or heard from in a long time. Don't get down on yourself for losing touch and don't (we repeat, *do not*) let this stop you from incorporating these contacts in your search. Reach out to long-lost friends. Life gets crazy; the situation could have easily been reversed, with your friend reaching out to you. The key is to not make it all about you. Be sure to ask about what your friend has been doing. Focus your discussion on rekindling an old friendship and not about getting something from him or her.

*I can't believe how long it's been since we chatted. How are you? I've been keeping up on your updates on LinkedIn. How are you enjoying your new role at* [new company]*?*

Ask a follow-up question like, *Does your new job have you traveling, or do you stay home primarily?* or *Are you working on any cool projects these days?*

*I was wondering if I could treat you to coffee* [or dinner] *sometime in the next few weeks. My career has taken a few exciting turns, and now I'm looking to move into an inside sales position. I'd love your advice on the industry and to find out how you've navigated it so successfully.*

Do not ask for a job, simply a meeting!

*If you're free, what works best for your schedule these days?*

## Generate Buzz with a Newsletter

If you are very proactive, you may opt to create what Katy Colvin, senior human resources business partner with Manhattan Associates, did during her job search: a newsletter!

While Katy described her newsletters to us as "a little cheesy," there is no arguing with success. Not only did she get hired as a result, but she also received rave reviews and stayed top-of-mind with her friends, family, and colleagues during a rough transition. Although Katy wrote very few months of newsletters before she ultimately landed a job, her creativity piqued so much interest that she still hears from recruiters about opportunities even though she is happily employed.

## EXHIBIT 2: KATY COLVIN'S NEWS, VIEWS, AND UPDATES

### Monthly Feature: The Fourth Month—Lessons Learned

Well, after four months I am getting used to my freedom throughout the day. I don't know if that's a good thing or a bad thing.

Lately I have been running around town meeting with fellow job seekers and attending networking events. I have especially been focusing on a lot of the "green" events in Atlanta. Luckily, the two founders of the Green Chamber of the South have allowed me to work with them in growing the Chamber. They have even given me the title of Program Director! It's not a full time job, but it's been keeping me busy and the support from the founders has really been wonderful.

Going on four months in my job search is tough. I thought I would definitely have a job by now, but it's just a tough market. Because of all of you, I'm way better off than most. I wanted to thank you all again for sending me all those HR job leads over the last month. It gives me hope knowing others are looking out for me as well. Like I said before, little things can make a big difference.

Here are a few of the things I've been doing in my job search and personal life to keep my spirits up during these uncertain times:

- I am still utilizing a scorecard system that rates each job search activity with a point system. My goal is to obtain 100 points a week. Check it out: Job Search Scorecard!
- I recently attended a Big Ten Networking event here in Atlanta and am looking forward to getting more involved in the Atlanta Chapter of the Indiana University Alumni Association. I have great memories of IU!
- I am looking into taking Excel courses and hope to have taken at least one by my next newsletter.
- I am working with the Green Chamber of the South.
- I'm still taking tango classes every week. Max and I went to a tango class in Piedmont Park on Saturday and it was a lot of fun. I highly recommend it!

Please let me know if I can ever be of assistance to any of you. You have all been just great!

### Target Companies

| | | | |
|---|---|---|---|
| Newell Rubber-maid Inc. | The Weather Channel | Porsche | Eli Lilly |
| Boys and Girls Club | Salvation Army HQ | Habitat for Humanity | Johnson & Johnson |
| Carter's | World Travel Partners Group | Careerbuilder.com | Ikea |
| Scientific Atlanta | Trader Joe's | Fox Theatre | Whole Foods |

### My Target Industries

As I mentioned before, it's all about networking to get your foot in the door at a company, so . . . if any of you know anyone at one of these companies, I would really appreciate a connection.

continued from page 25

**Katy's Monthly Inspirational Quotes:**

"Resolve never to quit, never to give up, no matter what the situation."
—Jack Nicklaus

"Enthusiasm spells the difference between mediocrity and accomplishment."
—Norman Vincent Peale

"We are what we repeatedly do. Excellence, therefore, is not an act but a habit."
—Aristotle

"Nothing will ever be attempted if all possible objections must first be overcome."
—Samuel Johnson

**A Few Upcoming Events:**

- Monster Career Fair—June 23
- Boys and Girls Club Summer Event—June 25
- Go Green Expo—June 26–28
- Viewing the first LEED certified factory-built home—July 1
- Green Chamber of the South Green Wednesdays Lunch—July 1
- 4th of July—Hope you have a wonderful celebration!

If your first inclination during your job-search campaign is to reach for a lifeline by shouting at the top of the highest mountain, "I need a job!" you're not alone. For a campaign that will yield greater results, a cautiously executed plan will do the trick. The expression "slow and steady wins the race" comes to mind here, as it's more effective to carefully communicate what you need from your network than to randomly ask everyone you know for help, leaving your network with no way to help you.

## Career Success Steps

- Secure a professional email address.
- Focus your job search on more narrow targets.
- Draft a Personal Marketing Plan to share with your network. See Exhibit 3: Blank Marketing Document on the next page for a place to start.
- Communicate your preferred jobs in the form of a PMP, rather than circulating your resume.

# EXHIBIT 3: PERSONAL MARKETING PLAN FOR _____

## Target Functions:

Title #1 _____

Title #2 _____

Title #3 _____

## Strengths:

- ■ _____
- ■ _____
- ■ _____

## Company Attributes:

- ■ _____
- ■ _____
- ■ _____

## Location:

First Choice City, State _____

Second Choice City, State _____

Third Choice City, State _____

## Target Companies and Industries:

Note: You may have fewer industries than shown below and more companies in each.

| Industry #1 | Industry #2 | Industry #3 |
|---|---|---|
| 1. | 1. | 1. |
| 2. | 2. | 2. |
| 3. | 3. | 3. |
| 4. | 4. | 4. |
| 5. | 5. | 5. |
| **Industry #4** | **Industry #5** | **Industry #6** |
| 1. | 1. | 1. |
| 2. | 2. | 2. |
| 3. | 3. | 3. |
| 4. | 4. | 4. |
| 5. | 5. | 5. |
| 6. | 6. | 6. |
| 7. | 7. | 7. |
| 8. | 8. | 8. |
| 9. | 9. | 9. |
| 10. | 10. | 10. |

# 4

# How to Cold Call

oes the idea of initiating a call to a hiring manager, recruiter, or someone else you'd like to meet send you into a cold sweat? We've watched talented, brilliant, knowledgeable experts be reduced to tears anticipating the rejection that often accompanies a cold call.

Although cold calling is considered old-school marketing, it still works—and don't let anyone tell you otherwise. In fact, the availability and popularity of social media have made collecting data, such as names, titles, companies, and interests, quicker and easier; people who were difficult (if not impossible) to find are now simply a phone call away. In the past, you had no choice but to rely on "May I speak with the head of marketing?"—which would rarely route you to the correct person. Now, with a little online research, you can correctly uncover the name of the head of marketing, ask for "Zaria Pecheco," and get transferred right to her.

There are various reasons for you to reach out to potential employers:

1. To request an in-person or phone informational interview (to determine if the job/company/career choice is right for you).
2. To follow up on an application you submitted, either in person or via the corporate website.
3. To follow up after a phone interview or an in-person interview.

Countless people stumble on the phone, or give up entirely, because they don't know exactly what to say. Cold calling works. It just takes courage and practice to incorporate it into your overall strategy and implement it with success.

Consider the following tips before embarking on a cold-calling campaign.

## Top Six Cold-Calling Techniques for Job Seekers

1. **Always get the name of the person.** Let's be clear: there is absolutely no reason for you to start a "smile and dial" campaign without first conducting some research and identifying your contact's name. Finding data about the person via LinkedIn, Twitter, or Google+ and uncovering key details will make your conversation more productive.
2. **Consider the time and day.** Not all times of day are created equal. Friday afternoon, for example, is not a good time to call, nor is six p.m., when an employer is likely hustling out of work to catch the metro or heading home to make dinner with her family. Morning is traditionally a good time to reach key influencers, as they are settling into the day, checking email, and drinking a morning latte, which often accompanies a spike in energy!

3. **Uncover company pain points in advance.** The more you know about the challenges the company may be facing, the better position you'll be in to influence someone to meet with you. If the company doesn't have a problem, or if you can't solve it, you have no business making the call in the first place. Make sure there is something in it for them—this is the way you can begin to sell yourself.

4. **Ditch the pleasantries.** Sure, it's important to appear cheerful and happy on the call, but don't expect the hiring manager to care if you are enjoying the weather today, so don't bother asking her. You called for a reason, so keep it short and succinct, and be respectful of the person's time. Establish whether or not it's a good time to talk and, if it is, share briefly why you are calling, and make a clear and confident request.

5. **Become allies with the phone gatekeepers.** Executive assistants, receptionists, and office managers like to play defense for the team they support, protecting their bosses from unnecessary interruptions. An authentic request such as: "I wonder if you would be willing to help me?" will go a long way toward getting a gatekeeper on your side. Be cordial. Develop strategies to work collaboratively to uncover information about the right person to contact or the best time of day to reach him/her. Don't forget: get the gatekeeper's name—and always be sure to thank him or her.

6. **Prepare a toolkit.** Maggie Mistal, certified life-purpose and career coach, says it best: "Soul search, then RE-SEARCH, before you job search." If the hiring manager asks you why you want to meet with him, and you reply, "I just really need to work right now," you've definitely missed an opportunity to sell yourself. Preparation is king.

Create and keep a written "cold-call toolkit" by your side when making calls to employers. In your toolkit: (a) your scripts, (b) any notes about the company you are calling, (c) your resume, (d) your calendar, (e) a pen and paper, and (f) a contact tracking sheet formatted for notes on the date, time, person, company, address, telephone, reason for calling, follow-up date, interview date/time, and comments. Or elect to use an automatic personal organizer as your tracking mechanism. JibberJobber, Fresh-Transition, and CareerShift get rave reviews and can make following up at appropriate intervals hassle free.

This due diligence on the front end will pay dividends as you competently and confidently make your calls.

# Types of Cold Calls

## Calling a Networking Contact with No Lead or Introduction

Here are a few scripts for requesting a meeting with a networking contact you do not know.

**Purpose:** Getting a meeting with your target employer to uncover information, share knowledge, and determine if the company/career field is a fit.

> *Hello, my name is Jasmine Brown, and I'm doing some research on working in _____. I found your profile on LinkedIn and it is quite impressive! I'm looking for some candid advice on how to break into the field, pros and cons of working in _____ , and how you successfully navigated the industry. Would you be willing to schedule a few minutes to talk when it is convenient for you?*

or

> *Hello, my name is Jasmine Brown, and I'm considering the possibility of working as a _____. I have been conducting some secondary research online and in the library, but there is only so much you can learn without talking to someone in the field. It would mean a lot to me to speak with you for a few minutes. I'd love to hear what it's really like to do this job on a day-to-day basis.*

or

*Hello, this is Jasmine Brown. I'm exploring the possibility of a career in _____ , but I don't know much more than what I've read in books and found online. Before I go any further, it would be so helpful to speak with someone who has done the job and can give me a realistic view of what to expect day-to-day. I found your profile on LinkedIn and you have such great experience. Would you be willing to speak with me for a few minutes next week?*

### Calling a Networking Contact with a Lead or Introduction

**Purpose:** When you know someone in common, it makes a cold call just a little warmer.

*Hello, Karen. Luis Gonzales suggested I speak with you about your experience in sales at Company X. He says you have done very well for yourself there, and thought I would benefit from speaking with you as I make my decision to change careers and move into sales. Would you be open to speaking with me briefly, over coffee perhaps?*

or

*Hello, Karen. A mutual friend, Luis Gonzales, urged me to reach out to you. He told me that you have been enjoying your experience at Company X and are doing well in hospitality management. I'd love an opportunity to speak with you about your experience, and your company, to determine if it could be a fit for me in the future. I'd love to take you for coffee or speak with you briefly at your convenience.* (Read more about the usefulness of informational interviews in Chapter 6.)

# How Often to Call

Imagine you are a hiring manager, perhaps at your desk conducting interviews, convening with a client, trying to wrap up your expenses from your recent trip abroad on business, or eating your brownie from the break room since you worked through lunch. Would you want to see the same number pop up on your phone, again and again, every 15 minutes? If you are like most managers in the United States, you are resource-constrained and trying to do a million things simultaneously. Picking up the phone to respond to an aggravating "phone stalker" who refuses to leave a message is not on the top of your list.

How much is too much when it comes to cold calling a company to request a meeting? You may be asking, "If calling every hour makes me look desperate, and not calling at all is not an option, how often is just right?" Great question. We call this the Goldilocks Principle, or the "just right" frequency to cold call an employer.

We posed this question to several managers on LinkedIn, and here's what they said:

- Locate your contact's email address and use it.
- Once a day is acceptable, but at some point, *please* consider leaving a message.
- If you've left a message and have not yet heard from us, you have permission to follow up once a week (if you are truly qualified).

## Follow Up!

Most candidates do not take this last step, but it can be what separates you from an interview and the resume black hole.

Chris Havrilla, recruitment and sourcing leader for Havrilla LLC, suggests the following after you've submitted a resume via a corporate website, and wish to follow up with a phone call:

"If you are truly qualified, I would follow up within 24 to 48 hours to reiterate your interest in the role. Most candidates do not take this second step, which will help you stand out, ensure your credentials are reviewed in a timely manner, and demonstrate your enthusiasm for the position and the company. My goal as a recruiter is to follow up with an applicant within one to two business days. However, since many recruiters carry requisition loads that make that kind of turnaround impossible, I would say a week is still reasonable. As a candidate, put yourself in a recruiter's shoes and recognize that he or she is doing their best."

According to an Accountemps survey, of the more than 1,000 senior managers at companies with more than 20 employees, 81% believe job seekers should not wait longer than two weeks to follow up. Interestingly, only 1% never want to hear from you! In other words, if you are not following up, you are probably leaving a job opportunity on the table.

In your follow-up call, use the following script as a guide:

*Good morning, Ms. Hyatt. My name is Jackie Rae, and late last week I applied for the marketing manager position your company posted on the AMA website. I want to confirm that you received my materials.*

You also want to take advantage of the fact that you have the recruiter on the phone, so prepare your pitch in advance. Focus your comments on the most unique and important aspect of the job description that best reflects your skills and abilities (highlighting, for example, your leadership and management skills would be too broad). For example:

*In the job description, it is clear that you are looking for someone with experience working in international markets, including China and Japan. I recently returned from a five-year stint in Japan, where I rolled out a new Sony mobile product. I hope you agree I would be a great fit for your organization. Can you tell me your time frame for next steps on this position?*

Leaving a brief phone message including your short pitch is appropriate if you cannot reach the recruiter.

Before you make your call, remember to Google your contact, review his or her credentials on LinkedIn, and analyze what comes up. Prepare a script and rehearse it a few times so you don't miss your chance to leave a powerful and compelling message.

## Leaving a Voicemail Message

Although hiring managers would prefer it, we do recognize that leaving a message puts the ball in the employer's court. If no one returns your call, you may feel rejected and uncertain about next steps. However, if you keep in mind that "less is more" when you leave your message, the hiring manager may be curious and call you back.

> *Good morning, Mr. Lee. I'm* [your name], *and I'm calling because I am working on a project I would love to get your expertise on. I will be in the office all day today. My number is* [number]. *Thanks, and I really look forward to speaking with you.*

*Note:* You don't mention your pitch, the fact you are a job seeker, or your credentials in this message. Leave just enough to pique their interest.

## You Reach Someone, but He/She Is Too Busy

There are times you'll get lucky and the person you are trying to reach picks up, but does not sound receptive to a conversation. If the person says he or she is too busy, address that feeling immediately.

> **You:** *I can be flexible to accommodate your schedule. If you like, we could meet early in the morning or late evening.*
> **Hiring manager:** *That's not going to work; I've got a lot on my plate over the next few weeks.*

> **You:** *I understand. If next month is better, that would be great for me as well. I could call a week out to confirm that it still works for you. I assure you that I won't take more than 20 minutes of your time.*

Even if the person does not want to speak with you, you can still capitalize on the conversation. Ask for a referral to a colleague in the same industry or a specific company.

> **You:** *I understand that you are very busy. Can you refer me to a direct report or a member on your team?* If they agree, ask, *May I tell them you referred me?*

## GETTING PAST GATEKEEPERS

According to job search expert and former recruitment firm owner Mary Elizabeth Bradford, known as "The Career Artisan," a great way to get past the gatekeeper is to use keywords such as "associations" or "networking" to get on the inside. The following are her suggestions to avoid being stymied by the gatekeeper.

### Refer to "Associations"

**The gatekeeper:** *Can I tell him what this call is regarding?*
**You:** *Certainly. It's regarding the Texas Chapter of the Associated General Contractors.*
**You can even add:** *I understand he is president, and I am contacting him regarding membership and my relocation to the Chicago area.*

### Refer to "Projects"

**You:** *Hi! This is ___ from ___. May I speak with Mr. Smith, please?*
**The gatekeeper:** *May I tell him what it is regarding?*
**You:** *It's regarding a project I am working on.*
**The gatekeeper:** *What kind of project?*
**You:** *A networking project.*

continued from page 37

## Refer to "Quotes"

Say you saw a quote recently in an article you read, as in the example below.

**The gatekeeper:** *Can I tell her what this is regarding?*

**You:** *Yes—it's regarding the new wind-farm project in North Texas.*

**The gatekeeper:** *What about it?* (Only a small minority will push the envelope like this.)

**You:** *I am working on a project, and I would like to talk to her about it.*

You see? And to add some rocket fuel to that, you would be wise to integrate something you saw or read into a compliment once you are talking to the contact:

**You:** *And by the way, I was really impressed to read about your focus and dedication to research technologies.*

If all else fails, and you are unable to get to the key influencer, Mary Elizabeth suggests asking:

**You:** *Does she have voicemail?*

or

**You:** *I'm sorry. It sounds like there is a problem. May I leave her a message on her voicemail at least?*

# Your Contact Does Not Remember You

On occasion, you may wish to reach out to a person you met a while back, who may not remember you. Call anyway, and use this script as a guideline:

**You:** *Hi,* [name of contact]. *This is* [your name]. *We met last year at the Power Women's Conference in San Antonio.*

Recall the camaraderie of the meeting. Share something memorable about your interaction with your colleague.

**You:** *I was the one handing out the chewy chocolate candies at our luncheon!*

**Your contact:** *Hmm . . . I'm not sure I recall it. It was really busy that day. What is this call in reference to?*

**You:** *I completely understand. We met a lot of people that weekend, but you stood out for me. I recall our conversation that day because you gave me some really great advice on the manufacturing industry that I truly appreciated. I'm exploring opportunities in this industry and was wondering if you would be open to setting up a 10-minute meeting with me. Your insider perspective is invaluable to me.*

As you've read, with the right preparation, cold calling is still a useful job-search strategy. Use a script in conjunction with a cold-calling campaign to open doors.

And yes, while cold calling can be very effective, there are still times when you will want to write, or leverage social media, first. Consider your comfort level with the various mediums, and look for cues via your research from the people and companies you are targeting before you choose a communication vehicle. If you can't get anyone on the phone, then cold calling isn't going to work: move on!

## Career Success Steps

Before you pick up the phone to reach out to that potential employer, do your research, build a script, practice it, and prepare for any possibility. Anticipate the circumstances that the hiring manager might be under before dialing, and put yourself in his or her shoes. Most importantly, don't let a sloppy voicemail message or surprise interference by a gatekeeper get between you and your next job. Use the following list to prepare.

Gather the important props prior to your cold call, including:

- Your scripts.
- Any notes and research about your contact and/or the company you are calling found via LinkedIn or an online search.

- Your resume.
- Your calendar.
- A pen and paper.
- A "contact tracking" sheet formatted for notes on the date, time, person, company, address, telephone number, reason for calling, follow-up date, interview date/time, and comments.

# How to Contact and Inform Potential References about Your Search

**M**ost job seekers spend so much time trying to land interviews, they fail to prepare for the inevitable next step—creating a list of references to provide a potential employer. These references serve as influencers and advocates. It is critical to be able to provide a list of contacts you believe are well qualified to endorse you, and who are eager to support your job application.

## Who Should Be on Your List?

Whenever possible, choose people who have witnessed your work firsthand. A current or immediate past supervisor is an ideal addition to your list, as their opinions tend to carry more weight than endorsements from colleagues or friends. If you cannot identify a supervisor to support you, choose co-workers, trusted subordinates, or clients. If you are a student or recent graduate, faculty members may serve as references. If you have had a volunteer leadership role, supervisors from that organization may offer a favorable perspective.

It's important to remember that employers don't always stick to the list you provide. All they need to do is Google you or your employer, or conduct a little research on LinkedIn to discover people who will be able to comment on your work. The only reference usually considered off-base (without your permission) is your current employer.

## HARD-COPY REFERENCES ARE EXTINCT

If you are a more experienced job seeker, you may remember asking people for letters of recommendation to keep on file when employers requested them. In today's litigious society, people are unlikely to put anything critical in writing. Today, employers prefer to speak to your endorsers directly to gauge interest, enthusiasm, and excitement about your candidacy, so it's usually not worth asking for hard-copy letters. (LinkedIn endorsements, which we discuss in Chapter 11, are the exception.)

# Asking Permission

Once you decide on your list of targeted references, ask for their permission. If they seem hesitant, allow them to bow out gracefully. You don't want to browbeat anyone into helping you. (They may hurt more than help.) The best references are enthusiastically supportive.

# Sample Email Asking Someone to Serve as a Reference

Dear *[former supervisor's name]*:

It's hard to believe it's been two years since we worked together! I'm glad we can keep in touch a bit via Facebook and LinkedIn. Have you gotten into Twitter yet? I'm just beginning to think it might be worthwhile; I'll keep you posted.

I haven't shared my job-search plans with anyone yet, but I did want to ask if you'd mind if I included your contact information on a list of references I am planning to put together; I am thinking about looking for a new opportunity. Things are going great at Company K, but it is pretty clear my boss is here for the long haul, and I'll need to find a new place if I ever want to move ahead with my own career plans.

Please let me know if that's okay with you, and also confirm that the following contact information is correct:

[List full contact information, including mailing address, email, and phone number.]

# Sample Inquiry to a Former Colleague When You Haven't Kept in Touch

If you have been out of work for a long time, William Holland, author of *Cracking the New Job Market: Seven Rules for Getting Hired in Any Economy* (AMACOM, 2012), suggests contacting your work references with the following type of email or note:

Martha, I'm in the job market and it's been a tough go. I'd like to put you down as a reference even though we worked together many years ago. I want to have a conversation about me and see if you're in a position to vouch for me and for the work I did for you. If you are, I'd like to bring you forward and talk about where I am now.

# Prepare Your References to Support You!

Once you have permission from several professional references, be sure to keep them up-to-date with the most recent version of your resume and a cover letter for your target jobs.

### Sample Letter Preparing Your References

Dear [former supervisor]:

Thanks so much for agreeing to serve as a reference for me. I'm attaching my current resume and listing links to my social resume (online profile), LinkedIn profile, and Twitter feed, just so you have a good idea of what I'm doing to market myself. Notice I've shifted my focus from marketing to sales, since I believe my best skills are in dealing directly with customers. Feel free to suggest any feedback on my materials and to let me know if you have questions. Thanks again so much for agreeing to be a reference for me. I will keep in touch as my search moves forward.

Sincerely,
Sari Marcus

## Asking Your References to Support Specific Details Regarding Your Candidacy

When it's time for hiring managers to call references, be sure to give them a heads-up and offer suggestions of topics you wish for them to emphasize. It's a good idea to send an email when you communicate specific details. That way, your reference has everything in writing and won't forget the important information:

Hello, Jill! I'm so excited to tell you I finally landed an interview for a job I'd really love. The meeting went well, and they mentioned they'll probably be checking my references next, so I wanted to touch base and fill you in on some details.

The job is a community manager for a visitors bureau in Tucson. In the interview, it was pretty clear they want someone with experience consulting with clients to help them achieve measurable results. They also really want to hire someone with a lot of experience customizing presentations to target stakeholders.

I hope you'll be able to support my candidacy on both points. As I know you'll remember, when we started working together, our biggest goal was to begin to show measurable changes in our social-media ROI. Using Google analytics in combination with a social-media action plan, I captured the data the board needed to see, and we increased site traffic by 25% in only three months. And did I ever customize presentations! Remember the decks I created for the community, for our colleagues, and then for the executive committee? It was so exciting when everyone was on board and we could move ahead with the plans.

I'm so grateful to have your help. I really appreciate the time you've taken to advise and assist me. Let me know if you have any questions! Have a great week, and hopefully you'll get a call from the Tucson Visitors Bureau soon.

Best,
Zachary

## SUCCESS STORY

When Miriam was applying for her job at Emory, she discovered in the interview that teamwork and a willingness to pitch in when necessary were crucial skills her employer was seeking. As soon as the interview ended, Miriam contacted her references, informed them of the employer's "hot button" issues, and asked them to emphasize her teamwork and willingness to pitch in when they spoke on her behalf.

Hopefully, you will have a strong relationship with your references and will feel comfortable making them partners in your search. Identifying and sharing key job requirements, buzzwords, and skills directly from the job description, such as "innovative" and "decision maker," with your references will enable them to effectively endorse you.

In the story above, by sharing specific details about the job, Miriam transformed her references into active advocates! When the hiring manager finished speaking with her references, he picked up the phone to offer Miriam the position!

## Keep in Touch with Your References

Sending emails, notes, and updates about your search are all great ways to stay in touch with the people who are key to helping you land the job of your choice. Set up Google alerts to be notified of anything Google indexes about your references. (Simply Google "Google alert" to learn how.) In doing so, you may discover that they earned a promotion or a new job, for example, and can quickly email a congratulatory note. Similarly, if you are connected via LinkedIn with your potential references, monitor LinkedIn network updates; if your references change jobs or make other announcements, you'll be notified and will have a chance to respond.

## Sample Thank-You Letter for a Recommendation Letter

Don't forget to say thank you when people spend their time supporting your job-search goals. It's important to express gratitude, even when the job doesn't work out.

Dear [recipient name],

I just wanted to thank you so much for writing such a thoughtful recommendation letter. As you know, I recently applied for the job of [position title] with Company B; it was an exciting interview process, and it came down to three candidates. The job ultimately went to someone with a few years more experience.

I remain optimistic about my job prospects as I continue my search. As you know, I'm anxious to get started in [industry], and I feel confident about two interviews I have scheduled over the next few weeks. It means so much to me to have your support during this transition period. I know your introductions and support will continue to play a significant role in helping me get invited for interviews.

If there is anything I can ever do for you, please don't hesitate to ask.

All the best,
[Your name]

# Career Success Steps

- Identify three to five references who will be willing to endorse you.
- Ask permission to use their names and confirm their correct contact information.
- Provide references with updated versions of your resume and other application materials, links to your social-media profiles, and copies of job descriptions after you interview and expect them to be contacted.
- When a prospective employer may be following up with your references, be sure to tell them how they can help convince the hiring manager you're the one for the job.
- Keep a list of people who are helping you and be sure to follow up with thank-you notes.
- Watch for news from people on your endorsement list so you can touch base if they have good news.

# How to Solicit, Secure, and Succeed at an Informational Interview

**A**n "informational interview" is a highly focused information-gathering session with a networking contact. The goal? To help you choose or refine your career path or learn something you could not otherwise uncover from online research. Ideally, you will access ideas and insights you might not have considered. One very important fact to remember—an informational interview has nothing to do with a job. *Don't ever ask for a job at these meetings.* Instead, use them to open doors for conversations with key influencers or other networking contacts and to gain clarity about your search.

⮑ **CAREER SUCCESS TIP**

During informational interviews, you ask the questions. Since your networking contact has no obligation to evaluate or rank you, he or she can chat freely, without pressure. If you play your cards right and ask meaningful, intelligent questions, you will learn about the person and his or her field or organization. One goal should be to gain a new ally; hopefully, your new contact will be inspired to help you.

You can win an informational interview through personal referral, written request, or cold-call telephone contact. When you ask for an informational interview, your inquiry should be concise, to-the-point, and broken down into sections:

- Establish your connection (if any) with the target contact.
- Showcase your relevant experience/education.
- Identify your goal in asking for an appointment.
- Make a very specific, straightforward request.

⮑ **CAREER SUCCESS TIP**

When you request an informational interview, don't send a resume along with your inquiry. There is no job on the table, only information.

## Request for an Informational Interview with an Old Colleague (with Whom You Did Not Stay in Touch)

As we discussed in Chapter 4, during your job-search campaign you may need to reach out to an old friend or colleague. Consider the following sample script, submitted by Kristin Johnson of Profession Direction, LLC, as inspiration.

1. **Establish your connection (if any) with the target contact.** Whenever possible, recall a conversation, story, or something meaningful to your contact. Don't just jump right into what you need or want; share a bit about your life and ask about him or her before you make your request.

   Hi [*name of friend*]! I bet you thought I'd fallen off the face of the earth! I'm so sorry I lost touch. I can't believe how much time has gone by, can you? I've been keeping track of your updates on LinkedIn and I see that you have a new job at [company]. I hope it's giving you the flexibility you were looking for when we last spoke. I'd love to hear how you are settling into your new role there and if you are enjoying it. Did you ever make it to China back in 2008?

2. **Showcase your relevant experience/education.** Let your contact know a little about you (or, in this case, what's been going on since you spoke), so she can make an informed decision about meeting with you.

   Quite a bit has changed on my end as well. Since our days at [*shared company*] I've worked at [new company], where I traveled abroad for six months. Since then, my career has taken some exciting turns, but I remain focused on a move into sales and am more passionate than ever about it. I never forgot your suggestion to join [sales association] and have been a member for two years now, and I love it. I know this is my time to make a move!

3. **Identify your goal in reaching out for an appointment.** Help is not a four-letter word (okay, you got us—it is, but not a bad one). Be clear about what you are looking for and how your contact can best help you. (Remember: it's not asking for a job.)

   I am writing because I would really appreciate your advice and help. I was wondering if you would be willing to review my resume and provide feedback on how you think I might be viewed within this industry. I'd love to discuss if there are any areas of my resume that you believe I should change, and if there is any reason at all you think I may not be considered a good candidate, at least on paper?

4. **Make a very specific, straightforward request for a 20- to 30-minute period.**

    Even though we haven't been in touch, you have been an important part of my life, and I value your expertise! I will call you on Friday to set up a lunch or coffee meeting. I'm looking forward to catching up.

# Asking for a Meeting without a Lead

Use this sample letter in your communications with a person at your target company to pave the way to future informational interviews.

Dear Dr. Barros [*find a name from LinkedIn, a trade journal, or via a Google search*],

It has been such a treat to read about [*company*] in the news recently! As an architecture student and intern at [*XYZ company*], I enjoyed following the press about your work and your new government contract. It certainly will be nice to have a city center within arm's reach!

As a student at [*school*], I am enthralled with cutting-edge companies like yours, and I have a strong desire to learn about the inner workings of [*company*]. I am proud to say, each semester I rank in the top of my class, a testament to how passionate I am about architecture and ongoing learning.

Although you have no openings right now for an architectural assistant, I would love the opportunity to meet with you briefly to learn more about your career, your company, and any corporate challenges and trends you might be facing. It would mean a lot to me to speak with you, even briefly.

I will call you on Tuesday morning at 10 a.m. to see if we can arrange a time. I look forward to our talk.

# Targeting Previous Employees of a Company

In your mission to land meetings at certain companies, you may come across a previous employee of a target company. Meetings of this nature can be extremely useful in helping you uncover essential information about culture, trends, and employees.

## *Networking Letter to Previous Employees of Your Target Company*

Elizabeth Craig, master career and job-search specialist with ELC Global, a career and lifework consultancy firm, shared this letter:

Dear Jane Doe, [*find name of person from local monthly business magazines, LinkedIn's advanced-search feature, local newspapers, chamber of commerce, college and university alumni associations, or contacts through fraternal and honorary organizations*]

It was terrific to see the feature article about you in the [university alumni association] newsletter. Congratulations! It was such a coincidence to read that you have previously worked for one of the companies I am interested in learning more about.

My specialty is in quality assurance, and I believe [*Company X*] may be a fit for me, but would really appreciate an opportunity to learn from you, as you worked there for a long time and appear to have had great success there. Would you be open to speaking with me briefly this coming week? I know you are busy and will call you on Tuesday at four p.m. to find a time that is convenient for you.

Thank you in advance for your assistance.

# What to Do Once You Have a Real Interview

Since informational interviews are exploratory and not about a job, once a specific job is posted or a company selects you for an actual interview, it's awkward to attempt to get in to meet with an unknown contact without making it about you and your career hopes. However, you may be able to find a contact who used to work at the company to share insights with you if you approach it correctly.

Joellyn Wittenstein Schwerdlin, known as the Career Success Coach, shared the following sample for job seekers who already have an interview scheduled and need some insider insights.

In the example below, Connie began a search for a warm lead within the Girl Scouts after they selected her to interview for a job. Her job-club leader, Joellyn, gave her Margaret's name and suggested they meet to help Connie gain a competitive advantage in the interview.

Dear Margaret,

My name is Connie Anderson and I'm in a job club facilitated by your friend Joellyn Schwerdlin. Every week, we discuss our job search and employment-interview progress. When I mentioned my upcoming interview with the Girl Scouts of Central/Western Massachusetts, Joellyn thought you might be able to help me. I understand you worked for this region for two years as a business-development consultant.

I'm being considered for the position of membership recruiter, which was recently advertised in the *Worcester Telegram & Gazette*. Of course, I'm very familiar with the Girl Scout mission. However, I would love to get an insider's perspective about the organization, which can possibly give me an edge at the interview.

With that said, I would like to invite you for coffee (my treat!) to discuss this further. Any help you can offer me would be greatly appreciated. I will call you early next week to set up a time.

## What to Ask in an Exploratory Informational Interview

If you are a student, career changer, or professional ready to identify the next best career choice, exploratory informational interviews are a wise way to uncover information about a job, industry, field, or company you are considering. You will also ascertain how people perceive you relative to that function, industry, or job target. Your underlying questions may include: "Do I have enough experience?" and "Am I missing a piece of expertise (software, certification, or accomplishment) necessary to be successful in this field?" If you are looking for honest feedback about how to position yourself as a right-fit candidate, exploratory informational interviews are your go-to tool.

As always, the mantra is "Be prepared." Determine what you need/want to know about the person you are meeting, and carve out appropriate questions to get at those answers.

Questions to ask come in various forms: company-specific questions, function-specific questions, industry-specific questions, and questions about the person you're meeting. (Don't forget—most people enjoy talking about themselves!)

## Company-Specific Questions

These questions are useful for uncovering information about corporate culture, challenges, and competitors:

- *What do you like most about this company?*
- *How does your company differ from its competitors?*
- *What does the company do to contribute to its employees' professional development?*
- *How does the company make use of technology for internal communication and outside marketing?*
- *What is a typical career path in this field or organization?*

## Company-Specific Questions for Unlocking the Corporate-Culture Mystery

When exploring a company of interest, it can be tricky to uncover clues about its corporate culture without coming right out and asking, "What's it like to work here?" There are other effective, and more subtle, ways of playing detective in these situations.

For example, determining a company's proclivity for what is often referred to as work/life balance or work/life fit—the degree to which a company respects and preserves your time away from the office—can be very challenging. For candidates, questions asking about this information are considered taboo. Candidates are ill-advised to inquire about flexibility in scheduling, especially when they are still trying to sell themselves to the company. However, in an informational situation, you may be able to learn useful details about the company's expectations.

## INVESTIGATING CORPORATE CULTURE

Cali Williams Yost, CEO of the Flex+Strategy Group/Work+Life Fit Inc. and author of *Work+Life: Finding the Fit That's Right for You* (Riverhead, 2004), suggests that during an interview, it's best to keep the conversation focused on work and how you will contribute to the company. However, in an informational interview there is not usually a job on the table for discussion, so it can feel more natural to pipe in about your personal life. Do so with caution. While there may not be an opening at the time of the meeting, be respectful of the session and treat it as you would an interview. For example, to uncover information about the standard hours you will be expected to work, she urges job seekers to say:

- *Can you describe a typical workday for me?*
- *Can you describe a typical workweek?*
- *Are there times of the year that are busier than others?* Or, if you are nonexempt: *Is overtime common? Is it expected? How is it handled?*

Cali suggests considering how eager you are to work for the company before you initiate a conversation about work/life fit.

If your answer is "Yes, this is my top target company," you might want to be more indirect with your questioning. If your answer is "No, I'm really more concerned with the right-fit company for me," you might want to consider a more direct line of questioning.

Is having the flexibility to manage your work/life balance to fit either day-to-day needs (e.g., coming in a little later if necessary or periodically working from home) or more formal constraints (e.g., a reduced sched-

continued from page 56

ule or working from home two specific days a week) a deal breaker for you? If your answer is "Yes, it's a deal breaker," you want to be more direct in your questioning; if it is not a deal breaker, you might want to be more indirect.

Once you establish your true goals going into the informational interview, here are some of Cali's suggestions for how to handle both the direct and indirect approaches.

## Indirect Line of Questioning

Use this approach if having the flexibility to manage your time would be a "nice to have" rather than a "need to have."

**Step 1:** To understand if people have flexibility in the hours they arrive to or leave the office or have the ability to telecommute periodically, ask:

*Are people able to work from home if they need to, or shift their hours every now and then, as long as the work gets done?*

What you want to listen for in the answer are the following cues to indicate flexibility does or does not exist.

Flexibility does exist:

- *If you have a doctor's appointment, a meeting at your kid's school, or the weather is bad, no problem.*
- *Everyone has a laptop or a mobile phone, so we can really work from anywhere.*
- *We don't care when you work or where you work, as long as the job gets done.*

Flexibility might be limited:

- *Hmm, not really.*
- *What do you mean?* It's pretty clear what you mean. If they don't know, you might want to drop it, especially if you need the job or flexibility isn't a deal breaker.
- *No, we like people in the office when they are supposed to be here.*

**Step 2:** Depending upon the answers you receive and how much more information you want, decide whether or not to go further with your line of questioning. To learn more about culture and to see if you are the right fit, you could chat with a couple of employees in the company, and ask them direct, work-focused questions to clarify what you previously heard about the support for, and availability of, flexibility.

*continued from page 57*

## Direct Line of Questioning

Cali suggests you use this line of questioning if having the flexibility to manage your work/life fit is a deal breaker.

**Step 1:** Get clear and specific about the type of flexibility you are interested in discussing.

**Step 2:** If you're interested in informal, day-to-day flexibility, then possible questions to ask include:

- *How much flexibility do people have in the way they work?*
- *Can people flex their hours or can they work from home periodically without too much difficulty?*
- *Can you give me some examples of what you've seen people do?*
- *Do most managers typically support that type of flexibility, or does it vary manager by manager?*
- *What type of technology do people get to support the flexibility they have?*

**Step 3:** If you're interested in a formal type of flexibility that officially changes how, when, or where you work outside of the normal business hours and location (e.g., a reduced schedule, the ability to work from home two specific days of the week), then possible questions to ask include:

- *Does the company allow people to propose a reduced schedule or a plan to work from home a couple of days a week? Is that common practice, or is it limited?*
- *What is the procedure you would follow to present a plan for some type of formal flexibility?*

As you can see, a discussion centered on work/life fit is less uncomfortable during an informational interview than it is during an interview for a real job.

## *Function-Specific Questions*

These questions are useful for exploring career choices or deciding between two similar positions.

- *How does a person progress in your field?*
- *What is a typical day like for you?*

- *What are the duties/functions/responsibilities of your job?*
- *What kinds of decisions do you make?*
- *What percentage of your time is spent doing what? Is your work constant?*
- *What are the various jobs in this field or organization?*
- *What is the best way to enter this occupation?*
- *What work-related values are strongest in this type of work (security, high income, variety, independence)?*

## Industry-Specific Questions

This line of questioning is helpful for uncovering where folks hang out, what they might be reading, and what challenges or opportunities are on the horizon for the industry. For example: *What do you like and not like about working in this industry? What sorts of changes are occurring in the industry?*

## TARGETING YOUR FIELD

Always keep in mind that some of your informational interview questions should target the industry or specific field where you'd like to work. Laura Gassner Otting's book *Transitioning to the Nonprofit Sector: Shifting Your Focus from the Bottom Line to a Better World* (Kaplan, 2007) highlights questions to ask if you're investigating a not-for-profit organization:

- *What brought you to this nonprofit and this mission area? In what ways has it lived up to your expectations? In what ways have you been disappointed?*
- *I read with great interest about how your organization is expanding programs into four new states. This is particularly interesting to me as an entrepreneur. Can you tell me about the funding challenges that poses and how, given current philanthropic trends, you are planning to handle them?*
- *Whom do you consider to be your competition for funding, for media, for members, etc.?*
- *What is the working atmosphere like here? Is this typical for the nonprofit sector in your experience?*

continued from page 59

- *What do you enjoy about working here, and what do you dislike?*
- *I notice that many of the staff here, like you, have business backgrounds. What difficulties did that pose for you when you came into the nonprofit sector? In what ways did it make things easier? (Or, conversely: I notice that few of the staff have business backgrounds and wonder how you feel about the ability of people to switch sectors?)*
- *Which skills, experiences, backgrounds, or personality types have you found to be most successful in your role? Which have not?*
- *How has this organization and your role changed since you've been here? In response to what? How does it need to continue to change?*
- *How would you assess my background, and where do you think I ought to focus my professional development to be successful in the type of position I seek?*
- *Do you have any words of wisdom, advice, or warning based on your experiences? What do you wish you knew when you started that you know now? Who else might have valuable insight and a good network of friends and colleagues?*
- *May I follow up with you as my job search evolves to keep you posted and get additional advice along the way?*

### Questions Specific to the Person You Are Meeting

These questions are the must-have questions of the day; it's critical to express an interest in the career/interests/goals of the person who has agreed to meet you, not just in his or her ability to help you.

- *If your job progresses as you like, what would be the next step in your career?*
- *Why did this type of work interest you and how did you get started?*
- *How did you get your job? What jobs and experiences have led you to your present position?*

- *What part of this job do you personally find most satisfying? Most challenging?*
- *Why did you decide to work for this company?*

# Prepare to Follow Up

Before you leave a meeting, look around and consider what you learned during your time there, as it will help you follow up thoughtfully. Is the culture casual? If so, an email response may be suitable. Is the company conservative (professional attire/suit and tie)? A handwritten note may impress more.

You may be asking, "But this is only an INFORMATIONAL interview. Why do I need to follow up?" Keep in mind: thoughtful follow-up shows your appreciation, helps you nurture the relationship, and keeps the door open for future conversations. Immediately following an informational interview, jot down notes about what transpired: topics covered, personal interests discussed, and promises made. If you learned about your contact's favorite restaurant, make it a point to touch base once you've had a chance to dine there.

Informational interviews are great tools to secure hard-to-find information about a company, its employees, or its culture. Take these as seriously as you would an interview; many times, they could prove to be launching pads to your successful job search.

## *Follow Up After an Informational Interview*

Dear [informational interview contact],

I just want to thank you for the opportunity to chat with you on Tuesday. I can't tell you how excited I am about what you shared about what you and your team are doing. I truly enjoyed our conversation and appreciate your candor about what it's like to work at [company]. I believe that it would be a good fit for me in the future.

I know how busy you are, and it means a great deal to me that you took time out of your schedule to meet with me. It is clear to me why you've done so well at your company.

I hope you have a great time on your trip to Argentina. While I've never been there before, I've heard that the alfajores are a delicious local snack!

I will be sure to keep you in the loop as I move through my research of target companies and in my job search.

To further nurture this relationship, follow up with your contact a month or two later, inquire about her trip to Argentina, or send a link to information you believe she would find interesting (perhaps about Argentina).

### Request a New, Warm Lead

There will be times when your best efforts won't land you in front of a hiring official, even when you've been referred by a friend or close colleague. In these instances, circle back and give the referrer a status update. Use this letter by Laurie Berenson, president of Sterling Career Concepts, LLC, to improve your chances of receiving another warm lead.

Dear David,

Thank you again for the time you took to speak with me two weeks ago, and I appreciate your thoughtfulness in passing on an additional contact name to me. Unfortunately, I've been unable to reach Mary. Do you have a suggestion as to how to best reach her, or do you know someone else in the client-service area with whom I could speak? I don't want to inconvenience Mary if this is a particularly busy time at work right now.

Thank you so much for any suggestions you might have.

## Career Success Steps

- Identify your goal in securing informational interviews. Is it to refine your career options? To determine if you are perceived at a high enough level for the job you want? Confirm if the career field is one you would enjoy, or if it would afford you the work/life balance you desire?

- Make a list of key influencers from your target companies who you'd like to meet. Research topics of interest to your prospective contacts using local monthly business magazines, chambers of commerce, college and university alumni associations, fraternal and honorary organizations, and LinkedIn's advanced-search feature, among other sources. (More on this in Chapter 11.)

- Craft your email (or phone script) for reaching out to contacts. Use the four-step guideline outlined in this chapter.

- Create a list of questions you'd like for your contact to answer. Your choices include function-specific questions, company-specific questions, industry-specific questions, and (most important for building a relationship) questions specific to the person you are meeting.

- Follow up thoughtfully to thank your contact and stay in touch; emailed letters are acceptable ONLY if you believe that the culture of the company would endorse an emailed thank-you note. If you believe the company or interviewer is a bit old school, follow up with a handwritten note or letter.

7

# How to Network at Events (and Make It Easy to Follow Up)

I f you feel awkward at in-person networking events, you are not alone. Even the most seasoned networker asks, "Where do I start? Who should I talk to? Do I have anything in my teeth?" Having some tricks in your back pocket should help you feel ready to face in-person networking events. As with everything pertaining to a job search, preparation is key.

## Be a Connector

To overcome anxiety, plan ahead to identify specific topics to discuss. Lynn Wong, a senior manager in global logistics at a Fortune 500 company, recommends that you think about how *you* can help others before you attend networking events. People generally perceive generous networkers—those who give before they expect to get—more favorably than those who only seem interested in talking about themselves.

Even when she attends events solo, knowing no one, Lynn acts as a "connector" and plays "host," first meeting people, then thoughtfully introducing them to each other when she thinks there may be a mutual benefit.

## Etiquette When Introducing People

A bit of introduction protocol may be helpful, since we tend to approach social situations informally. Etiquette calls for introducing the "lesser-ranking" person—either professionally, socially, by age, or seniority—to the "higher-ranking" person.

1. State the name of the higher-ranking person.
2. Say, "I would like to introduce."
3. State the name of the person being introduced (or the lower-ranking person).

Note: Peer-to-peer introductions follow no special protocol.

A few examples:

**Introduce a junior professional to a more senior one.** *Mr. Levi* [a marketing director], *I would like to introduce Scott Pennsley, a recent graduate of Brooklyn College.*

**Introduce a host to a guest.** *Elana, I don't think you have met my daughter, Joni. Joni arranged for all the food at this festival. Elana is my project manager.*

**Introduce a client to your boss.** *Mr. Client, I would like to introduce you to my manager, Mr. Jones. Mr. Jones, this is Robert Client, vice president of XYZ Corporation.*

**Introduce a high-ranking official or person of special prominence to a friend or colleague.** *Bishop Gordon, may I present my husband, John?*

**Introduce a peer from your company to a peer from another organization.** *Vera and Sam, I would like to introduce you to each* *other. I believe you could have some synergies in your businesses, as you both run the H.R. departments of your respective companies.*

When initiating introductions, keep these rules of thumb in mind out of respect for title and accomplishments and to avoid offending anyone who is a stickler for protocol.

## Outside-of-the-Box Conversation Starters

Think about touch points that connect us all, but that *don't* necessarily have anything to do with work. In particular, focus on what you might have to offer. Lynn advises collecting ideas, resources, or advice that you can have at the ready to suggest to help someone else. While this may initially feel forced, the more you practice these conversation starters, the more comfortable you will be using them.

- Can you hook up contacts with a terrific bartender for their party?
- Do you know someone who can paint a mural for a new nursery?
- Do you know of a great place to get the best wings in town?
- Do you have a favorite recipe to share?
- Have you heard of an awesome place to get discounted tickets, or a hot vacation spot?
- Do you have any terrific websites, apps, or online resources to suggest?

People appreciate someone who offers to help. Promising the name of a contact or specific information is a great lead-in when you want to connect after the event.

### Be a Resource
Being a valuable resource to others can lead to you becoming the "go-to" person in your niche or community. Lynn notes, "This role

pays you back many times because others begin to seek you out to share ideas and connections. Good people beget good people." For her, go-giving is a way of life, and is not simply restricted to sharing contacts on LinkedIn or swapping business cards.

## Sample Introductions

Introducing people at networking events provides a great launching pad for building strong connections and will help you continue and nurture the conversation after the party is over. When you meet people at networking parties, at the park, or in the supermarket, steer the conversations to a topic that enables you to connect on a personal level.

See how many of these topics Mya works into a conversation starting with an innocuous mention about the weather. (Assume the conversation began with all the usual niceties.)

> **Mya:** *It's so hot out today . . . Can you believe this weather?*
> **Kris:** *Seriously . . . I've never seen it so hot here.*
> **Mya:** *I'm not from here, are you?*
> **Kris:** *No, I was actually born in France.*
> **Mya:** *Really? Where in France are you from? How long have you lived in the States?*
> **Kris:** *I'd say about 15 years or so . . . We moved here from Eze for my wife's job, and I really like it. Except for the wine!*
> **Mya:** *Ah . . . So, you're a wine connoisseur?*
> **Kris:** *Being from France, it's all about the pairings!*
> **Mya:** *Have you ever been to Vino? They have wine and cheese tastings once in a while.*
> **Kris:** *No, never heard of it. I'll have to keep an eye out!*
> **Mya:** *It's nice to meet you . . . Let's keep in touch!*
> [Exchange cards]

In this conversation, Mya created several potential "hooks" to help her reconnect with Kris. For example, she could touch base about news or information about France, but the wine interest is a perfect future connecting point. Not only can Mya send a note about the next event at Vino (and even invite Kris and his wife to join her), but she can also send wine-related articles or other events of interest.

## ⮂ CAREER SUCCESS TIP

Unless you work in a politically or religiously oriented field, it's best to avoid those topics. Don't assume anyone will agree with, or want to hear, your views. It's best to play it safe and touch on other personal subjects, such as hobbies or sports affiliations.

Here's a sample script focusing on sports. Notice how Jon and Bill don't have to root for the same team for their conversation to generate good follow-up fodder!

**Jon:** *Are you planning to watch the Braves game tonight?*
**Bill:** *No, I'm not much of a fan.*
**Jon:** *Do you have a different favorite sport?*
**Bill:** *I don't miss a Florida State game . . . My wife even had to rearrange our twins' first birthday party because I couldn't miss a big game.*

Depending on his interest, Jon can now either follow up about Bill's twins (maybe he has young kids of his own) or his sports fanaticism. Either provides a great future touch point.

In the next scenario, Genie learns about a hobby of Rosemary's, despite the conversation's initial slow start.

**Genie:** *Hello, I'm Genie Appel.*
**Rosemary:** *Rosemary Micet, nice to meet you. Where do you work?*
**Genie:** *I'm a human resources staffing expert. I know how to find the right talent to solve a company's problems and keep them*

*on the road to success. In fact, I've just completed a project and am looking for a new opportunity. How about you?*

**Rosemary:** *Funny coincidence—I'm also in HR. I work on training and development at XYZ Company. So many people are looking for work now. We've laid a lot of people off at my organization. It's pretty depressing.*

**Genie:** *I can imagine. It's not easy to be left after a layoff, but it's probably not as bad as looking for a job in this economy!*

**Rosemary:** *I just hate these networking things, don't you?*

**Genie:** *You know, they say networking is how most people find jobs, so I do my best to stay positive. What do you enjoy doing when you're not working?*

**Rosemary:** *Actually, I'm a big gardener . . . I raise orchids. It's really rewarding!*

**Genie:** *Wow, I don't know anything about orchids . . . Is it hard work?*

**Rosemary:** *It can be. There's a lot to learn, but I'm a member of a club here in town, and it can be relaxing to focus on something other than work.*

**Genie:** *I bet it is. Oh, it looks like they're going to start the program soon, but I would love to continue this conversation. Do you mind if I touch base with you on LinkedIn? I'd like to be in contact.*

**Rosemary:** *Sure, feel free to send me a note.*

In Genie and Rosemary's interaction, Genie could have thrown in the towel early on rather than pursue a connection. If you, like Genie, make it a point to identify at least one item to use as a hook to follow up with promising prospects, you'll be well prepared to do so with grace and sincerity.

With a little effort, you can easily identify articles or blog posts about the topics that interest your new contacts. When you share those resources, you help ensure they don't forget about you. (See Chapter 8 for a sample follow-up note from this conversation.)

# Career Success Steps

Even if you dread approaching strangers or are uncomfortable in new environments, practicing and preparing things to discuss will make it easier for you to meet and get to know people you want to include in your network. Take our word for it: if you complete this to-do list, you will be ready to work the room!

## *General Preparation*

1. List topics you enjoy discussing and would be comfortable bringing up in a networking conversation. List at least five things you're an expert at or you enjoy.
2. List some current books, movies, and magazines you intend to learn about before you attend your next networking meeting to stay up-to-date on current events.
3. Visit www.alltop.com to identify some blogs in topics of general interest. Bloggers are usually up-to-date on the most topical information—you should be, too! Find 5 to 10 blogs in your professional niche you'll plan to review regularly. Try to choose frequently updated blogs written by authorities or leaders in your field.
4. Consider setting up an RSS-feed reader to collect and organize your favorite blogs. Visit http://www.squidoo.com/rss-explained to learn all about RSS and how to create a reader.
5. Make a list of questions to engage new contacts, including open-ended inquiries that allow people to talk about themselves.

## *Before Attending an Event*

1. Read the magazines and blogs you identified. Have something to say about sports standings, movies, books, and/ or the news.

2. Identify three to five movies or books you can discuss.
3. Research who is planning to attend the event. Review the organization's information and use LinkedIn's Events application.
4. List what you know about the top three people you hope to meet.
5. What do you hope to learn from those three people (personally and/or professionally)?

## After the Event

Search Google for recent articles or news pertaining to your new contacts' interests. For greater efficiency, set a Google alert (an automatic notification) of information indexed about relevant topics. (To learn how, just search Google for {Google Alert}.) For example, if you need a great post on orchids, Google will notify you via email when it finds something new.

Identifying topics of interest to you and your prospective contacts will help ease any discomfort or fear you may experience in networking settings and better prepare you to make meaningful contacts.

# 8

# Post-Networking Event Follow-Up

**S**etting the stage for easy follow-up is one important step toward managing your career and controlling your own professional path. Many job seekers underestimate how important it is to follow up. There are three main types of post-networking event follow-up we'll cover in this chapter: follow-up via written notes and email, phone calls, and social networking. This chapter provides a series of ideas incorporating all three styles, with examples from a variety of situations, including:

- You met casually in person and created a follow-up hook (as described in Chapter 7).
- You met, but did not have a true conversation.
- You met briefly and have a mutual contact.
- You met a potential mentor.
- You are following up after a career fair.
- You are thanking the event organizer.

# Written Follow-Up

There are several general rules of thumb to consider when writing networking letters. Most written communication is electronic. However, in some cases a mailed letter may be more appropriate; for example, if you have not heard back from an email and cannot reach the person on the phone, or if you have reason to believe your contact will appreciate a formal note. Regardless of the delivery, written follow-up should respect the following rules:

- **Be succinct.** Most people are busy and don't have a lot of time to decipher a long note about why you are writing.
- **Do not include a resume** or mention your job search unless the person specifically asked for it. When networking, emphasize only your quest for information; do not mention a job. (The exception to this rule is if you are contacting a recruiter or hiring manager after meeting at a career fair.)
- **Incorporate something you know about the person** or ask something to help make a connection. (See Chapter 7 for examples of how to collect information during your meeting to use for following up.)
- **Remind the person about your interaction.** For example: *I was the tall guy wearing a White Sox tie.* Or: *I hope you remember our heated conversation debating the merits of the Kindle Fire compared to the iPad.*
- **Be sure to mention a mutual connection, if there is one.**
- **State when you will follow up by phone, if applicable.**

# Telephone Follow-Up

Usually you will reserve using the phone for a secondary follow-up contact, but it's perfectly acceptable to call someone without writing a note if you believe you made a strong in-person impression. The challenge most job seekers encounter with the phone is determining the best time to call, what to say, and how to move things to the next level, as phone conversations can be so unpredictable. In these cases, practicing will help you overcome objections you might encounter during a call. (See Chapter 5 to learn how to make cold calls. In this chapter, we'll suggest what to say when you have met the contact before.)

Things to keep in mind before you follow up on the phone:

- If you say you're planning to call the person in a certain number of days or weeks, do it!
- Call early or late in the day (but not *too* early or *too* late!) because those are the times when you are most likely to reach your contact.
- Make a few notes about what you want to say. Focus on your target goal—if you want to ask for a meeting or something specific, make sure you do so before ending the call.
- Choose a quiet place, and try to use a phone unlikely to drop the call.
- Always ask if it is a good time to speak.
- As outlined in Chapter 6 in the discussion about asking for informational meetings, avoid asking for a job. Remember— you are following up to solidify or continue a professional relationship, not to get something from the contact. (The exception is when you do have a particular favor to ask. Just make sure you never ask for a job.)
- If the person is unwilling or unable to help you, ask for a referral. Be sure to ask if it is okay to use his or her name when contacting the referral.
- Always have a positive attitude and be sure to thank the person, even if the result was not what you intended. Keep communication lines open.

# Following Up Using Social Media

We've dedicated several chapters to outlining how to best communicate, engage, and create professional relationships using social media tools, especially LinkedIn, Twitter, Facebook, and Google+. This chapter includes examples demonstrating how easy it is to combine social media tools with more traditional approaches.

- Following up via social networking requires a little research and sleuthing; go the extra mile to locate someone's LinkedIn, Twitter, or Google+ accounts. (Resources in the chapters dedicated to those tools later in this book will help you find people on those networks.)
- Consider social media interactions as you would written or telephone ones: always be polite, remind the contact when and where you met, and make an effort to establish a reason to extend the relationship.
- If you don't hear back via the social media tool, it is possible that your contact does not actively use or monitor communication from the network. Or he or she may choose to visit and respond to inquiries to connect only once a week or several times per month. Don't get discouraged! Gently incorporate the three-pronged approach (written, telephone, and social-media follow-up) to identify and connect with people who reciprocate your interest.

## Following Up After Casually Meeting In Person When You Created a Hook

Don't miss out on potential relationships. Complete the career success steps in Chapter 7 to improve the quality of your networking interactions. The following are examples of how to follow up after one of the scenarios described in Chapter 7.

## Social Media Follow-Up

Genie follows up with Rosemary via a LinkedIn invitation. (You can read about their meeting in Chapter 7.)

Dear Rosemary:

I really enjoyed our talk this week at Re:Focus on Careers. I hope you'll agree it would be nice to keep in touch via LinkedIn, since we're both in human resources. I hope we can meet again soon. Please don't hesitate to be in touch if I can introduce you to someone in my network. And, not sure if you are aware of this, but there is a LinkedIn Group called "Flowers in Nature" devoted to flower and nature lovers! Here's the link: _____.

Sincerely,

Genie Appel

## Written Follow-Up

Here is a sample follow-up letter:

Dear Rosemary:

It was great meeting you last month at the Re:Focus on Careers event in Buckhead! I hope things are looking up at your company after all of the layoffs. I know sometimes it's tough to be one of the last ones standing. When we talked, you mentioned you raise orchids. Coincidentally, I came across this article in the *New York Times* about a master gardener in Rhode Island who maintains one of the oldest species of orchids in the country. Here's the link: _____.

I'm glad we're connected via LinkedIn. I hope you'll keep me in mind if you happen to hear of any opportunities where my employment-relations skills would be put to good use.

I am looking forward to a chance to see you at another event soon. I hope you don't mind if I touch base in a month or two via phone. Enjoy the holiday weekend!

Sincerely,

Genie Appel

## Telephone Follow-Up

**Genie:** *Hello, Rosemary. It's Genie. We met a month and a half ago at the Re:Focus on Careers event in Buckhead . . . I'm the one who sent you the link to that story in the* New York Times *about the orchid gardener. Is this a good time to reach you?*

**Rosemary:** *Hi, Genie! Sure. It's good to hear from you. I remember you . . . I hope you got my email thanking you for the article?*

**Genie:** *I did, thanks! I had mentioned I planned to give you a call. Have things settled down at work after all the layoffs? You must be pretty busy.*

**Rosemary:** *A little bit . . . We are keeping our fingers crossed that we may be looking for some contract help after the new year. Right now, it is pretty hectic.*

**Genie:** *That is great news! I wanted to touch base to ask if you were planning to attend the end-of-the-year Re:Focus event next week?*

**Rosemary:** *No, I have so much to do with the holidays coming up, I'm going to skip this one.*

**Genie:** *That's too bad. It's a really busy season, that's for sure. Those events are so hectic, anyway. Would you be willing to meet for coffee in the new year? I really value your opinion and expertise and would love to ask for your advice about my job hunt. Maybe you'd be willing to go over my resume with me and make some suggestions?*

**Rosemary:** *Hmmm . . . I'd really like to help, but, you know, we don't have any opportunities at my organization . . .*

**Genie:** *Of course! I understand you don't have any jobs available. I am getting my marketing documents in order and could really use your wisdom. If you're not TOO busy, maybe just for 20 minutes or so next month?*

**Rosemary:** *Okay. How about January 8? Around 2:30?*

**Genie:** *Perfect! Thank you so much. I really appreciate you taking the time. I'll send you a follow-up email.*

# You Met, but Did Not Have a True Conversation

In a formal networking setting, you will speak to a lot of people, but likely will not have in-depth conversations with all of them. You may even return home with a stack of business cards from people you don't even remember! Upon reviewing the business cards, if you realize someone works at one of your target companies . . . it's time to do a little sleuthing.

Search on LinkedIn for the person's profile or Google his or her name and title. You should be able to find photos and profiles to help jog your memory and fill in missing details.

## Follow-Up Note or Email

Dear Benjamin,

We both attended the CFA meeting at Sage Restaurant last night, but it was so crowded, we hardly had a chance to speak. I'm sorry I missed the opportunity to touch base with you in person, but I've sent a LinkedIn invitation, and I hope you'll be willing to "link in" with me.

Will you be attending next month's meeting at Maraca's? I'm planning on being there and hope to have a chance to meet and speak with you then. I'll plan to touch base with you in the middle of the month.

Sincerely,

Selena McKavoy

## Social Media Follow-Up

When you saw the person but didn't really get a chance to connect, it's perfectly acceptable to extend your fleeting interaction via social media. For example, search Twitter or Google+ to gauge their online activity. (See Chapters 12 and 14 to learn how to find them.)

If, for example, Benjamin uses Twitter regularly and tweeted about attending the event at Sage, follow him on Twitter. Then follow up in public with a tweet such as this:

@BenjaminCFA I wish we had a chance to speak at the networking event last night at Sage, but I am looking forward to following your tweets and connecting here on Twitter.

An engaged Twitter user who is open to networking will probably follow you back and may even respond:

@SelenaMC Nice to see you. Hope to catch up with you at another CFA event soon.

Review Chapter 12 to learn many more ways to engage and interact with networking contacts using Twitter.

# When You Met and Have a Mutual Contact

### Follow-Up Note or Email

Dear Matthew,

I enjoyed our brief conversation at last night's American Red Cross fundraiser. I couldn't believe how many items they had up for the silent auction! Congratulations on coming home with the electronic keyboard—it looked like a great instrument.

Even though we didn't have a chance to have an in-depth conversation, my friend Michelle Burns made a point to say I should reach out to you because we have so much in common, both having worked as consultants and Mets fans, to boot!

I'll send you an invitation to connect on LinkedIn, but I hope you'll be up for a coffee or lunch meeting sometime soon. I'll give you a call early next week to try to see if we can coordinate schedules.

Sincerely,

Steven Missert

## Follow-Up Phone Call

You're not always going to be lucky enough to reach someone when they are available to speak to you. Don't let it discourage you from following up.

> **Steven:** *Hi, Matthew . . . This is Steven Missert; we met last week at the American Red Cross fundraiser. We have a mutual friend, Michelle Burns.*
>
> **Matthew:** *Hey . . . I got your note. It's been a busy week!*
>
> **Steven:** *I know what you mean. Do you have a minute now to talk?*
>
> **Matthew:** *You know, I am about to go into a meeting. Can you call me Friday morning, before 10?*
>
> **Steven:** *Sure, no problem. I'll touch base then. Speak to you soon.*

## Social Media Follow-Up

Always mention the person who connects you if you have a mutual friend or contact when connecting on LinkedIn:

Dear Matthew:

I'm glad we had a chance to touch base at the American Red Cross fundraiser. Our mutual friend, Michelle Burns, suggested I be sure to follow up with you, as she thinks we have a lot in common. I hope you'll agree to connect here on LinkedIn. Please don't hesitate to let me know if I can make any introductions to people in my network. Speak to you soon.

Sincerely,

Steven Missert

# When You Met a Potential Mentor

Occasionally you have an opportunity to meet a potential mentor or a prominent member of your organization or field. (Be sure to review Chapter 9 about connecting with VIPs.) Most people probably will not follow up after such a meeting; you might be surprised by how often an opportunity extended from a significant networking contact does not garner a response. Don't let that happen to you. If you meet a great connection who offers to be in touch with you, be sure to respond quickly. (Note how the following message demonstrates how useful it is to have exchanged some personal details.)

## Follow-Up Note or Email

Dear Dr. Havens:

It was a real pleasure meeting you at the University of Miami's student/alumni event last night. It was so nice of you to take time from your busy schedule to come to campus to meet students like me. As I mentioned, I am a big fan of your work, and I've read all of your books.

Thank you so much for offering to get together for coffee to tell me the backstory behind your latest book. I have classes all day on Mondays, Wednesdays, and Fridays, but I am completely free on Tuesdays and most Thursdays.

I will give you a call in two weeks after you've had a chance to catch up from your vacation. Enjoy the Grand Canyon!

Sincerely,

Yousef Mehta

## Follow-Up Phone Call

**Yousef:** *Hello, Dr. Havens? It's Yousef Mehta; we met at the U. of M. alumni event the week before you went on vacation.*

**Dr. Havens:** *Right! How are you?*

**Yousef:** *I'm doing well, thanks. Did I catch you at a good time? I know how busy it is after coming back from vacation.*

**Dr. Havens:** *Yes ... I got back last week, and I am just catching up.*

**Yousef:** *It was so generous of you to offer to meet me to talk about your latest book. Do you think you'll still have time to meet up for coffee sometime soon?*

**Dr. Havens:** *Okay. Sure. You mentioned there were certain days you are free?*

**Yousef:** *Tuesdays and Thursdays are very flexible for me.*

**Dr. Havens:** *Why don't we give me another week to get things settled and we can meet on the 15th?*

**Yousef:** *That is perfect. Is there a time and place most convenient for you?*

**Dr. Havens:** *How about 1:30 at the Corner Café on Fifth and Vine?*

**Yousef:** *Great. I appreciate it. I'll send you an email next week to confirm our plans.*

# When You Met at a Career Fair

Remember, when you meet at a career fair, you are free to send your resume and mention your interest in a job (just this once!).

## *Follow-Up Note or Email*

Dear Ms. Maxwell:

Thank you very much for taking the time to attend the career fair sponsored by the University of Iowa's career center. It was a pleasure meeting you, and I was excited to learn that [organization name] is looking for new hires who have strong writing skills and experience managing events and speaking in public. My background is an exact match!

As we discussed, as an English major with a separate focus in communications, I've been active in a variety of literary magazines on campus and actually started a new journal about public relations, Full PR Press [include a hyperlink]. We're now in our second year, and we even have paid subscribers!

In my other free time, I am the events coordinator for Volunteer Iowa, the largest student volunteer organization in the country! I oversee four major events per year and coordinate teams of other student volunteers. A big part of this role is speaking to donor groups and large audiences of students to encourage them to participate. In fact, our membership has grown by 15% since I took the helm in the spring, and charitable giving has increased by 8%, even in this difficult economy.

As you requested, I am attaching a copy of my resume, and I also completed your online application for entry-level applicants. Please feel free to call [include your phone number] or email to schedule an interview. I look forward to the opportunity to meet with you again to discuss how I may be able to contribute at [organization name].

Sincerely,

Olivia Bajesti

### Social Media Follow-Up

If a recruiter includes his or her social media contact information on a business card, that is your green light to reach out via these tools.

Here's a sample LinkedIn invitation:

Ms. Maxwell:

We met at the University of Iowa's career fair this week. I'm so glad you attended and just submitted my application for an entry-level position. I hope you'll connect with me here on LinkedIn; I look forward to hearing from you soon.

Sincerely,

Olivia Bajesti

If the recruiter is on Google+ or Twitter, connect there, too. If he or she posts something relevant to your professional interests, comment intelligently. Be sure to "like" the organization's Facebook page if there is one, and don't forget to look for a careers page on Facebook if the company maintains one.

## Thank-You Note to the Host of a Networking Event

Everyone appreciates being thanked. Distinguish yourself with a brief note to someone who organized an event you attended.

Dear Tegan,

I wanted to let you know how much I enjoyed the Hiring for Hope event last night. It was an amazing opportunity to connect with employers, and I was so impressed by the number of committed "Angel" volunteers you brought to advise job seekers. I got some great advice about how to update my resume, and I now know I need to jump on the social media bandwagon to help get my name out there.

I can only imagine how much work went into putting together such a terrific and valuable event. Thank you so much for your hard work; I want you to know you're making a big difference to unemployed folks out there!

Sincerely,

Abraham Asaad

# Career Success Steps

Regardless of the method you choose, keep these tips in mind:

- Don't delay. Follow up as soon as possible after you meet. That does NOT mean you have permission to send a text message as soon as you leave the event! Generally, texting is *not* considered a tool that professional networkers use.
- After you leave a networking event, make a prioritized list. Which contacts are most likely to be receptive to your follow-up? Who offered to introduce you to someone? Was anyone working at a company where you'd like to apply? Focus your efforts on your best contacts first, in case you lose steam or run out of time before you reach out to everyone.
- If you collected business cards or used smart-phone applications to exchange information, be sure to write notes about the most promising contacts. Try to recall your conversations and the follow-up hooks you planted. Track these details so you will benefit from those meetings.
- When you get home from networking meetings, find your contacts on social media.

# 9 How to Reach VIPs

et's face it. To a certain extent, everyone you encounter during a job search is a VIP. No one can give you a crystal ball so you'll know if the woman standing in line at the grocery checkout lane or the man cheering at your kids' soccer game will lead you to a new opportunity, but it is a real possibility. Everyone you meet has VIP potential, but some people are arguably more influential than others—either due to clout, visibility, or popularity. These "important people" field more requests than they can reasonably answer, and as a result will likely position more gatekeepers between you and them.

But don't let that scare you. You can do it!

With social media tools becoming the norm in professional communication, you have more options now than ever to engage directly with VIPs. If an email or follow-up phone call fails, or you cannot find a mutual contact to introduce you, you can always turn to low-barrier methods such as Twitter or Google+ to interact directly.

# ADVICE FROM A TALENT AGENT

In recent years, the idea of hiring a professional advocate to speak to target companies on your behalf, especially at the beginning of your job search, has picked up steam. Debra Feldman, an executive talent agent with JobWhiz.com, is an ambassador who helps job seekers get past the corporate gatekeepers. Below are key phrases Debra keeps in her back pocket that have never failed her in "disarming administrative assistants and corporate receptionists." Likewise, she notes, the following scripts "transform them from gatekeepers to greeters!"

*Hello, this is Debra Feldman and you don't know me. I am trying to reach Ms. Jones to tell her [something very technically detailed to demonstrate that I have extremely complex knowledge, boosting my creditability and secretly implying that there is a bigger risk in diverting me than putting me through to the contact].*

*Hi, is this Mr. Smith, Ms. Jones's assistant? I am so glad that I was able to reach you directly. I have a message for Ms. Jones and am hoping that you will be kind enough to pass it along to her. Would you mind giving me either her email address or your own so I can send it to you to pass along to her when it's convenient? Great! Then I'll give you a call in a few days to confirm that you received it. It is really nice of you to help me reach Ms. Jones. I know both of you are very busy, so I won't be wasting any of your or Ms. Jones's time with this. Thank you again!*

*Hi, is this the XYZ private agency operator? My name is Debra Feldman; what's yours? Hello, Hannah. I'm calling to talk to Ms. Jones. We met at a recent conference where she was presenting [or: where I was speaking, and where our mutual friend, Mr. Frost, introduced us. He recommended that I call Ms. Jones]. Would you please put me through to Ms. Jones's line? Oh, okay, I understand. How do you recommend I arrange to speak to her on the phone? May I have her email address so that I can send her some information? In that case, may I send this to you and ask you to please pass this on to her?*

Debra asserts, "The key is to be cooperative, patient, and friendly. Do not get on the bad side of the gatekeeper. Your goal is to ingratiate yourself so that they use their status and knowledge to help you, rather than thwart your efforts and prevent you from achieving your goal."

# Define Your Goals and What You Offer

Identify your goals and what you hope to accomplish before you start your campaign. Even if you have easy access to someone with a lot of clout, it's best to wait until you have a firm plan in place and are ready to make the best use of the person's time before reaching out.

Don't target people just because they are "bigwigs." In most cases, you will be able to receive exactly the information and resources you need by speaking to someone only one or two levels above you. If you are absolutely certain that you must meet with a hard-to-access VIP, take a breath, get your game face on, and get ready to outline your specific plan. You'll need perseverance, strong research skills, and commitment.

The ancient Greek aphorism "know thyself" is very apropos here. Before you do anything, make sure you know what you offer the VIP. And don't forget, it must be unique. VIPs have lots of job seekers knocking at their doors (not to mention a host of their own employees and others vying for their time), so what you offer has to make them sit up and take notice.

Ask yourself:

- What do I offer the VIP that he or she can't get elsewhere?
- Is there a problem that I can solve?
- Do I have information, resources, advice, or a new perspective to share?
- Why is my inquiry intriguing?

This self-reflection will yield huge dividends in the end. Don't short change your progress by sidestepping this key to-do list.

# Invest in Your VIP

Internationally recognized etiquette expert and founder of the Protocol School of Palm Beach, Jacqueline Whitmore, is the author of

*Poised for Success* (St. Martin's Press, 2011). She notes, "Your correspondence or conversation [with a VIP] will flow more smoothly if you know something about her hobbies or interests." In the same vein, she suggests researching the VIPs passions before making a request. For example, read anything the person you want to meet has recommended reading. You'll also want to be up-to-date with what he or she writes (including a blog, Twitter feed, or newsletter) and stay abreast of what others are saying about it.

Additionally, Jacqueline explains, "You may need to stretch your budget to gain access to a VIP, especially if you desire to meet him/her in person." She cautions, "It's too brazen to put him/her on the spot or to corner someone (which will likely end with a security escort, anyway) when he/she is not ready to listen. Timing is everything."

## Make a Request (but Make It Snappy)

Mark Suster, an entrepreneur turned venture capitalist, blogged advice about why it's not a good idea to ask a busy person to lunch. Mark cautions, "Busy execs hate lunches. They are time sucks. Sure, they like to occasionally meet good friends for lunch. But somebody they don't know? Not so much." Instead Mark recommends asking for coffee, and even better if it's at their office. He urges job seekers to say, "Hey, can I bring you coffee and get 30 minutes of your time at your office next Tuesday or Wednesday? I promise I won't overrun my time." When you keep your promise, Mark says, "you become an easy second date to accept."

Mark's rule of thumb? "If you're asking for the meeting, you travel. If I meet somebody super senior—even if they've asked me for the meeting—I still travel. I want them to be the least amount inconvenienced. I want the meeting. I want it to be easy for them to have it. I'm the primary beneficiary."

Mark is not advocating that job seekers kill lunch entirely! In fact, he says, "by all means 'lunch,' but keep in mind with whom you're meeting, their level, the business they are in, and how well you know them to determine if it's even appropriate to ask. And," he suggests, "if you're slightly out of your league in asking them, start with a soft ask—'How about coffee?'—followed by a cheeky 'If you're open for breakfast or lunch, maybe we could grab a quick bite.' You'll notice in every ask I use the word 'quick.' It feels like less of a commitment."

# Get Introduced

Not surprisingly, the best way to successfully access a VIP is with an introduction. When identifying target contacts, start your quest by taking inventory of who you already know who can help you make inroads to the VIP with social media tools, especially LinkedIn, making it easy to research potential links between you and the person. Build a (metaphoric) bridge to your prospective contacts, and consider how many degrees separate you before trying to get in touch with them directly.

### *The Email with a cc:*

Once you identify someone who might introduce you, make a strong case for the referral. When an intermediary agrees to facilitate an introduction for you, Marci Alboher, a vice president for Encore.org and a self-professed "congenital connector," advises you to ask if you can open copy—or cc:—him or her when you email the VIP. Marci says that in a perfect world, your contact will use the opportunity to respond to everyone via email with a brief, enthusiastic endorsement, suggesting the target person respond to your message. This is a wonderful way to help you accomplish your goal of meeting the person you'd like to know and also lighten the load for your busy intermediary, who now can simply shoot off a quick endorsement, convincing the contact to respond to you.

Here's how it would look in practice:

**You (speaking to a potential intermediary):** *I was researching literacy in LinkedIn's skills area (Don't ask me how I got there, because I don't remember!). I found a page dedicated to this skill and a bunch of people, groups, and companies associated or related to it. Kathy Pratt is one of the people listed, and I read her blog regularly and, of course, have read her* New York Times *best-selling book. I was so thrilled to see that you are connected to her! As you probably know, I'm re-entering the field of literacy, and the topics in her book, especially regarding children and the national literacy rate, have me so intrigued about what can be done. I would love the opportunity to ask her how she conducted her research for the book (which I've read now three times and recommended to all of my friends). Would you be willing to share her email address with me so that I may reach out to her?*

**Intermediary:** *Absolutely. Kathy has been so busy lately, but I'm sure she'd love to hear how much you love the book and are putting it to use in your field. I agree—email is the best way to touch base with her. I'll forward her email address to you right now.*

**You:** *Thank you so much. Do you mind if I cc: you on the email I send to her? That way you can quickly send a reply to both of us recommending that she touch base with me.*

What if your intermediary does not offer the email address right away and offers to just email a note about you? While it's terrific that she wants to help, even some of the best intentions do not materialize, and when the time comes to remind her to do what she promised, it may be awkward. Instead, use the following script to walk away with something more tangible:

**You:** *I know you are so busy, too. How would you feel about giving me her email address? That way I can email her directly, copy you on the email, and you can quickly send a reply to both of us recommending that she touch base with me. Will that work?*

*Note:* In all of these scenarios, if you sense that your connector is hedging, back off. It is safe to assume that he or she isn't confident about getting the other person's opt-in. If that is the case, move on to a different intermediary or consider contacting the person directly via social media tools. (We include details about how to leverage social media later in the book.)

## ⤷ CAREER SUCCESS TIP

Let your work speak for you before you even make the connection. When you reach out via email, a signature line with links can be an ally, enabling the busy VIP access to your passions and expertise through the blog posts, creative works, quotes, news, and bookmarks you share. One tool that gets high marks from job seekers is WiseStamp, which empowers your email signature on any webmail service (Gmail, Yahoo! Mail, AOL, Hotmail, and Google apps).

### *Sample Email with a cc: to Your Mutual Contact*

Dear Tom [cc: Hal],

Congratulations on your new promotion to chief operations officer. It comes at an exciting time, too, with the 25th company anniversary coming up this June!

Our mutual friend, Hal, suggested that I reach out to you. Since the acquisition last year of Virtek Laser Edge, I've noticed that the company, under your direction, has been contemplating an expansion into the health care industry, an area I know quite a bit about. As a medical practitioner turned business owner (after a quick jaunt to an MBA program), I've been intrigued about what you do, and how laser templating can affect the medical industry at large.

I know you are extremely busy, but after you settle in, I would love to speak with you briefly. I think it could be very exciting to see what comes out of our conversation.

Sincerely,
Sanjay Mehta
Medical Consultant
Tel: 202-555-5555
Email: smehta@verizon.net
Read my new book
*Medicine in the Jungle*: www.medicineinthejungle.com

Ideally, Hal, the mutual contact, will "reply to all" with an email such as:

Dear Tom—I'm so glad Sanjay is reaching out to you. He was such a terrific asset to our medical practice before the business closed down, and I know the two of you would both benefit from meeting. I wholeheartedly encourage you to touch base!

## Connecting Directly with VIPs

### *Use LinkedIn*

LinkedIn is a terrific way to communicate freely with a VIP, so visit the VIP's profile and scour it for useful information. Where did she go to school? Does her profile display the books she is reading? Look to see if there is information in the "causes I care about" section. Check to see if you know anyone connected to the users who have recommended the VIP as a possible contact point. It's also acceptable to ask the VIP directly for a LinkedIn connection, but only if you have a compelling reason to link in (and if it's beneficial for your contact, not just for you). For example, in the script below, the author shares a group with a VIP. To connect, LinkedIn offers the opportunity to choose a mutual group. Once he selects the group, LinkedIn will allow him to ask for a connection. Make your reason to connect compelling and succinct:

*We've never met, but I noticed you mentioned in Forbes your company's intent to move into green architecture. I just spent three years studying this topic at the University of Colorado. I'm happy to be in touch if I can assist you in any way, and I hope you will agree to connect here on LinkedIn!*

Nothing beats establishing rapport, and LinkedIn offers a variety of ways to do so (e.g., groups, answers, updates, etc.).

## Use Twitter

It's not difficult to use Twitter to build relationships, even with highly visible personalities. Farhana Rahman, global social-media manager for Kitt Digital and author of the blog Social Media Coolness, offered the following tricks of the trade to help reach "top dogs" (including those you don't yet know) via Twitter.

### Be Persistent and Unique

Farhana once realized it was Om Malik's birthday. @Om, who has more than one million followers on Twitter, is the founder of GigaOm and a venture partner at True Ventures. She remembers fondly, "Of course everyone all over the world was tweeting him birthday wishes, but I decided to be different, and I tweeted him a 'Poem for Om.' He was so flattered—he thanked me twice, and followed me back within a few minutes!"

### Don't Treat the VIP Like a Rock Star

To cut through all of the Twitter noise, Farhana advises her network to "be regular" when vying for the attention of a superstar. She says, "Surely @InfluencerIvy must regularly deal with people trying to impress her, flirt with her, spam her, pitch her . . . it probably gets overwhelming! The way to grab her attention is to just *be regular*! It's kind of like those scenes in the movies where the whole crowd is going berserk, but you notice that one person who is calm and quiet. Be that one person who doesn't appear to be a leecher, or preacher, or creeper. I usually make the first move by commenting on a VIPs bio in an engaging way, and including their name to make it more personal." For example:

> @InfluencerIvy Hi Ivy! I would have NEVER guessed that a hotshot like you also bakes wicked cookies! I'd like some toffee please.

She would also ask totally out-of-the-ordinary questions, such as:

> @InfluencerIvy Ivy . . . would my cookies come out weird if I use mystery flour from the dollar store?

Farhana says that creative mentions such as these typically yield a response within one to two days.

Clearly it's possible to get someone's attention on Twitter, or even Google+ (using similar approaches). Remember, once someone follows you back on Twitter, you can send a private message. Depending on your goals, you may want to send a private message to acknowledge the person and continue the existing conversation. For example, once Ivy followed her back, Farhana could have messaged:

> I'm looking forward to sharing news about [whatever her field is] and to securing more of your cookie recipes!

Keep the tone conversational, even if you are freaking out that someone on your target list mentioned you on Twitter!

## Leverage Leadership Roles

We've all seen ads or commercials that admit, "These results are not typical." While it is possible to land a meeting using these targeted techniques, in some cases, persistence and creativity alone may not yield the results you want. Connecting to a VIP is easier if you can offer something of value in return. For example, if you are an active member of the Chamber of Commerce, on the planning team of your alumni association, or very involved in your national professional association, you may be able to create opportunities for the VIP by making new introductions, which is a valuable commodity.

## COMPLIMENT CREATIVELY

When you do want to compliment a VIP, Mark Stelzner, founder and principal of Inflexion Advisors and a respected and active thought leader in the HR community, suggests, "Instead of directly complimenting her, find an indirect means to achieve the same end. For example, if the organization recently expanded into Asia, you might mention '. . . how well the APAC growth strategy has been perceived by the market.' Since the CEO likely led the charge, the message, and compliment, will land."

Christine Comaford is an executive coach at Christine Comaford, LLC, and the author of *Rules for Renegades* (McGraw-Hill, 2007). She relayed a story on Forbes.com about how, 18 years ago, she convinced Steve Jobs to meet with her. Christine explains, "I sent a FedEx letter. Then I sent another. Then I started calling. Then I sent another FedEx, and called some more. Finally, after 7 FedExes and 12 phone calls, Steve's assistant said he wanted to talk with me."

Christine remembered his reply. He said, "You keep sending FedExes and calling. So let's end it. What do you want?" She retorted, "Five minutes of your time. I really admire your accomplishments and as a young CEO I have a few questions no one else can answer." "Bring a timer." "I will. Oh—and thanks." He had already hung up.

She described the meeting, where she brought a "chunky, white, metal kitchen timer" and asked questions that were "mere prompts to get Steve talking." When their five minutes was up, Jobs insisted they continue the meeting, which gave him an opportunity to wax eloquent on his vision for the future of computers.

Christine suggests the following three steps to help you land a meeting with any VIP in your life:

1. Find out what causes the VIP cares about. Write a genuine letter, no more than one page, about the specific accomplishments of the VIP you admire. Offer five hours' donation of your time to his or her favorite nonprofit for five minutes of the VIPs time (request an in-person meeting versus a phone call).
2. Send your letter via FedEx. Call to ensure it was received and bond with the executive assistant. Only call first thing in the morning or at the end of the day. The VIP is more likely to answer then.
3. Repeat step two until you get a meeting. If for some reason this doesn't work, give the letter to the VIP by hand at an event he or she is speaking at. Then repeat step two until you get a meeting. In 30 years in business, the approach above has always worked for me. The key is the letter. Be authentic, heartfelt, compelling. Care. Make it a work of art.

What should this letter say? Here are some hooks to capture the reader's attention. Stretch your imagination and do a lot of research to identify door openers. For example:

continued from page 97

- Do you share an alma mater? If you went to the same college or high school, you may have a better chance of a reply.
- Did you grow up in the same neighborhood? Perhaps a story about mutual friends you had or a favorite restaurant or hangout will appeal to your target.
- Is the VIP a rabid fan of a particular team? It's possible you may have a shared passion for sports to connect on. (Or highlight a shared passion for any eclectic subject: gardening, the opera, playing the violin.)
- Might the person enjoy flattery or humor? This could be a long shot, but some people respond to a quirky letter, and you could stand out in the crowd if you hit the right chord.
- Think about how you can help the person. What do you offer? Identify a problem you could solve or share a way to drive revenue to his or her firm, and you may earn an in-person audience.

## Sample Letter to a VIP

Dear Chris,

My name is Jonathan Bernard, and we met briefly at a charity event in Baltimore last fall. I am on the membership committee for [organization name]. My role on the board is to secure funds to provide programming and support for sustainability efforts in the D.C. area. I am fortunate to serve alongside talented community members who may be familiar to you: DeShawn Lewis, Lisa Applegate, and P'ninah Liu.

I haven't yet had the opportunity to speak with you, but I'm hoping we can fix that. I know of your significant presence in the community, and my organization is aware of your role in helping to improve the lives of children, both domestically and abroad, through your volunteer efforts. I'd love to see if there is someone to whom I can connect you on our board who may help with your corporate or personal goals.

I know you are an extremely busy person with very little extra time, so I would not take up much of it! I'd love the opportunity to meet with you for 15–30 minutes. I'll follow up with Elena [the assistant whose name you've already uncovered] about getting that scheduled.

All the best,
Jonathan Bernard

# Career Success Steps

- Before you reach out to the VIP, consider two things: What do you want, and what do you have to offer? Write two lists.
- When determining what you want, ask yourself: Is this VIP the only person who can help me? If so, craft notes about why this person is your "only hope." Then research this person as if it were your job. (That includes reading his or her favorite books or blogs.)
- Set Google alerts to locate recent PR and search social media sites to determine your VIP's passions, interests, and goals.
- If your target writes a blog, uses Twitter or Google+, or has a public Facebook presence, be sure to keep a close watch on all of these networks. When appropriate, comment and engage with the VIP via these networks.
- Use LinkedIn and other networking tools to identify mutual connections. If you don't have a connection, think about how you can create one. This may mean joining online groups, volunteering, or attending events where you will be able to meet potential liaisons.
- If all else fails, weigh options to connect with the VIP directly. This could include joining a mutual LinkedIn group; engaging on Twitter, Facebook, or Google+; offering to donate time to the person's favorite charity; writing a personal letter to send via FedEx; or hand-delivering a note to the VIP at an event.
- Once you gain access to your VIP, do not be greedy. Offer to deliver the coffee, guarantee a "quick" meeting, and don't beat around the bush. Get to the point about why you called the meeting.
- Wash, rinse, repeat. Stand strong. Have fortitude to keep up the work, even if it takes some time.

# 10

# How to Communicate Online: A Primer for Using Social Media

**S**ocial media tools such as LinkedIn, Twitter, Facebook, and Google+ (which we profile in the following chapters) can help you:

- Learn what leaders in your industry are thinking and writing about, even if you are not currently working in your field.
- Meet new people and expand your network beyond what you could ever achieve with in-person networking alone.
- Demonstrate your expertise, so people know what (and how much) you know and how you can help them solve their problems.
- Be found, so you can reverse the job-search process from a "push" marketing perspective—where you are applying for positions—to a "pull" marketing approach, making it easy for people to identify and contact you. When you set up

your social networking profiles well, they act as magnets, helping attract potential hiring managers to you.

> **↪ CAREER SUCCESS TIP**
>
> When you communicate online, always think about giving first. How can you be generous and provide useful information to your digital community? Online networking is all about giving.

# What Should I Say?

One common question about social media is "How will I know what to say?" It is a lot easier than you may think. Once you identify your niche (the topic in which you will be able to demonstrate expertise), it is easy to research and identify places to find information to share with your growing online community.

In each chapter dedicated to the networks we recommend you use, we include specific examples of what to say and how to say it. Here are some considerations to think about before you start:

**Identify what you want people to know about your expertise, and focus on how to showcase that information in your updates.** For example, if your expertise is in accounting, you can write about laws affecting your industry. This type of update would be appropriate for any social-media platform:

*Interesting article in the* Wall Street Journal *showcasing new standards for accounting* [include link].

If you are an administrative assistant, include data and information on productivity and organizational tips. For example:

*Have you seen the latest Thermal Label Printer? Includes new productivity-enhancing features* [include link].

Try to gear your updates around professionally focused themes. Get people thinking, "I need to keep up with her updates because she sends a consistent stream of information I need to know."

**Comment on the news of the day as it relates to your industry.** For example, if you are in health administration, an update (in any social network) may read:

*Learn how the new health care plan will affect your organization* [include link to an article detailing more information].

Or, if you are a teacher, a useful update (found via the news) might be:

*How one woman single-handedly reversed an inner-city school's outlook* [include link].

These can be the easiest updates to share because they come directly from the news. Track several reputable national and local news sources to keep in the loop. (You can follow these sources from within any of the networks—learn how in each of the following chapters.)

**Read books.** Make a list of hot books relevant to your field and showcase them in your updates. Comment on the content and invite discussion. For example, you may post:

*"Everything I Know about Business I Learned from the Grateful Dead," by Barnes & Perry Barlow, is a superb blend of humor and smart business principles that just makes sense.*

**Ask and answer questions.** Find questions via LinkedIn's Answers (this feature is explained more in Chapter 11). You can certainly answer the questions there, but there's no rule against taking them outside one network to pose in another. Either ask or reply to the question via your favorite social-networking platform. If you are using Google+ or Facebook, you can create a more extensive comment than on Twitter or LinkedIn.

**Read blogs and respond via your updates.** It's a good idea to identify and spend time reading blogs about your field. When you do, you'll have an unending stream of information to share with your online community. You can simply tweet or post links to the blogs you like, or you can comment on the posts in your updates. For example:

*Really enjoyed this post about lessons on leadership for consultants.* [include link].

This type of update would be appropriate on any network.

# HOW TO IDENTIFY BLOGS TO READ

When you hone in on key contacts, browse their LinkedIn profiles to see if they also write a blog. Anyone serious about blogging will include a link to the blog in his or her LinkedIn profile.

Using social media exposes you to a lot of different contacts, who probably also blog. For example, just perusing Google+ or Twitter feeds will help you identify new bloggers you may enjoy following. Once you have a good list of blogs, it will be much easier to create valuable and useful updates for your online communities, even if you choose not to blog yourself. If you use Google+, you can click through to Sparks, or "what's hot" and then insert a search term, and you'll see recent updates about the topic. This allows you to find blogs written about a topic you'd like to know more about.

More resources for finding blogs to read:

- Alltop.com: A magazine rack of blogs, this site categorizes numerous topics and provides easy access to blogs in your targeted niche.
- Google blog search (http://blogsearch.google.com/): A site that searches blogs.
- Google alerts: Google allows you to track subjects or keywords and receive email alerts when it indexes something relevant. Go to http://www.google.com/alerts to set up alerts that will no doubt include content from many blogs.
- Blog rolls: Many blogs have a blog roll, or a list of links to recommended blogs. Typically the blogs will be in a related niche. If you enjoy one blog, it's likely that the blogs the writer recommends will appeal to you, too.
- Twitter: Many people who tweet also maintain a blog. Follow the link from a person's Twitter profile to learn about the blog. Most links your Twitter friends share are probably to blogs you may find useful.
- Google: Enter {best blogs, topic} in Google, where the topic is your area of expertise. For example, {best blogs, accounting} yields several results, including the top 50 blogs for accountants.
- Technorati.com: Select Blog instead of Post at the top, and type your search-term topic. Technorati provides a list ordered by authority, a measure of a blog's standing and influence in the blogosphere.

*continued from page 104*

■ StumbleUpon.com: This site uses a ratings system to create a collaborative opinion about a site's value. StumbleUpon provides a list of almost 500 topics, and you can select your interests and potentially be matched with other people's suggestions.

## Comment on Blog Posts

While you may be reading blogs to give you fodder to post on your profiles, commenting on blog posts individually is a wonderful way to communicate your expertise. Avoid banal, uninteresting comments, such as "I really agree with what you are saying here." Instead, add some insight and offer your expertise.

For example, the following is an example of how Miriam responded to a post by Penelope Trunk at blog.penelopetrunk.com. The post was promoting Penelope's blogging boot camp. Miriam used this opportunity to share a bit of her own expertise and showcase her first book. (Your comments don't need to be so in-depth; shorter comments can get you noticed, too. Review other comments on the blog and consider creating a reply whose length suits the audience.)

*As you note, it's so important to make a distinction between earning a living BY blogging (which is for the very few) and using blogging to enhance and extend your career and business opportunities (which is available to anyone with writing skills, expertise in their field, and the willingness to follow through). In my book,* Social Networking for Career Success *(LearningExpress, 2011), I explain how blogging can be an important part of a social media strategy. As you note, it provides the blogger a platform to demonstrate expertise beyond what he or she can show in a resume, for example. You were generous enough to contribute some tips for the book, which was perfect, since I learned to blog, in part, by reading your blogs almost four years ago! I can't think of a better way for careerists (job seekers and small-business owners) to "show, don't tell" what they know. Blogging can allow people a place to illustrate how their skills make them well qualified to take on the positions or gigs they are targeting. Point #5 (blogging builds your network) is so important, and often overlooked. The more people who know, like, and trust you, the better off you are when it comes to landing opportunities.*

*When it's so important to distinguish yourself from everyone else, blogging (when done well) and being able to create a community of colleagues via a blog and other social media tools can mean the difference between being found or being lost in the shuffle.*

## Career Success Steps

- Don't forget—always focus on what message you want to push out via social media. Remain focused on your keywords. Answer the questions: *What do I want people to know about me? What do I offer that is special or unique?*
- Once you know your answer, you'll see that this entire chapter is a series of steps to help you succeed using social media. Keep them in mind as you consider how to use each social network to your advantage.

# 11 How to Communicate via LinkedIn

L et's not beat around the bush. There are two categories of job seekers: those who are serious about their job search and those who are not. If you are not on LinkedIn, you are firmly in the latter category. Being on LinkedIn is the "cost of doing business," especially these days, and if you choose to have no presence on this platform, you risk putting your job search at a serious disadvantage.

This platform offers limitless possibilities for you to connect about work and job-search topics. With such a profound viral ability to connect with people you know (and those you don't), LinkedIn is an essential component of your job hunt and the one tool we implore you not to do without.

On LinkedIn you can:

**Learn what thought leaders in your industry are thinking and writing about.** LinkedIn offers many opportunities to find out what people in your field are focused on. As described later in this chapter, you can review your contacts' profile updates and track and review updates from your extended network. Looking at the Answers section provides ongoing fodder about what people are asking and sharing.

**Meet new people and expand your network.** LinkedIn recommends that you connect with people you already know, but it's very easy to engage with and meet new people via LinkedIn. The Groups feature is particularly useful in this regard, as you have an opportunity to participate in discussions and online conversations with new people. Once you've exchanged several messages, it makes sense to consider asking for a connection. LinkedIn also allows you to ask for connections through common intermediaries (or common connections). This is a wonderful way to expand your network via referrals.

**Demonstrate your expertise.** LinkedIn allows you to showcase what you know by making profile updates, participating in groups, using the Answers feature, and highlighting your blog, Twitter account, and PowerPoint presentations, just to name a few. When you make an effort to use LinkedIn interactively, you will find a multitude of opportunities to show what you know, attract attention, and, ultimately, land jobs.

**Be found.** When you set up your social networking profiles well, they act as magnets that attract potential hiring managers to *you*. LinkedIn is considered a high-authority website according to Google, which means it is optimized to share your information with Google. Assuming you maintain open privacy settings to allow it to work well, it's likely your LinkedIn profile will be the first result people will see when they Google you.

As with all social networks, if you are generous on LinkedIn, you will add connections faster, create more meaningful connections, and propel your job search forward. Before we outline the do's and don'ts of LinkedIn-communication etiquette, we want to share the best way to succeed on LinkedIn *without really trying*. We'll boil it down to this: Remember your kindergarten rules. Play nice in the sandbox. Be kind. Think first about the needs of others. Be generous. Give, give, and give some more.

# Your Professional Headline

With professionals joining LinkedIn at a rate that is faster than two new members per second, it's more crucial than ever to build a compelling and zippy profile that differentiates you from the masses. This will require some "zing," and it all starts with your headline. According to Susan Guarneri, known as the Career Assessment Goddess, your headline goes hand in hand with your other personal-branding materials and should be used to "define who you are in a sentence." This concept, according to Susan, "arms job seekers with the confidence to talk about how they are special in an interview."

Your headline serves as your marketing slogan. (For example: "Nobody doesn't like Sara Lee" or Microsoft's "Where do you want to go today?") It must be memorable, powerful, and intriguing. Keep in mind that your name and professional headline are the only two things displayed from your profile when you contribute to a discussion via Groups or answer questions in the Answers section.

## *Three Tips to Consider When Creating Your LinkedIn Headline*

The headline field is capped at 120 characters. You do not have to include your job title.

1. **Identify your target audience.** To whom do you provide value (Is it universities? Fortune 500 accounting departments?) If you are unsure, ask yourself, "Whom do I want to attract with my message?"
2. **Consider the value you provide.** Be specific and narrow your focus whenever possible. This is known as your Unique Selling Proposition, or USP. Ask people you trust what they would say about what you do well. For example, are you the organizational maven? The go-to HR process expert? Marketer to small medical practices? Be sure to include your unique value (or *pitch*) in your headline.

3. **Make it memorable.** Be creative so that your headline will leave an indelible mark on readers. Add humor, if it fits your personality, but avoid making it cheesy or overly self-promotional.

**Organizational Maven for Fortune 500 Companies**

*I streamline your processes, so you can make more money*

## WHEN YOU DON'T HAVE A JOB

When in transition, you have two options for your professional headline on LinkedIn, says Jason Alba, author of I'm on LinkedIn—Now What??? (Happy About, 2012) and founder of JibberJobber.com, a tool for job seekers to organize the job hunt and manage a professional network.

**Option 1:** Lay your cards on the table.

*Project manager in transition, looking for my next role in the NYC area*

or

*Looking for new opportunities as a project manager with rich software-development experience*

**Option 2:** Be the professional you are (regardless of your employment status).

*Project-management professional providing exceptional value to large-scale software projects across multiple industries*

or

*Project manager (PMP), actively involved in multiple NYC PMI chapters—experienced in high-tech funded startups*

Jason says, "In option one, it is clear you are looking for your next gig—nothing wrong with that. In the second option, it is clear you are a competent professional (not that the first option doesn't portray that)."

D.C.-based social media consultant (and former job seeker) Yolanda Arrington took a different spin on her profile while in transition. In her headline, she removes the jargon and touts what she can do for you:

### Social Media Guru

*Need it produced, social media marketed, tweeted, Facebooked or written? I can take care of that . . .*

Regardless of employment status, Susan Guarneri insists that headlines should pack a punch like these below:

### Director of Corporate Communications

*Delivering consistent on-brand corporate communications with a personal touch*

### National Sales Manager

*Rainmaker and sales-team spark bringing $95 million in software sales in 10 years*

### Turnaround CEO—Trade Associations

*Transformative change agent who delivers results when it matters most*

### Senior Civil Engineer

*Systems maximizer who integrates projects, data, and people for quality results*

## Extreme Makeover for Your LinkedIn Summary

Walter Akana, career and life strategist at Threshold Consulting and co-developer (along with Carol Ross) of the Online Remarkable Profile, explains, "Too many people rely on their resume summary or a professional third-person bio to create a LinkedIn summary. Unfortunately, these tend not to be engaging or differentiating. Carol and I believe that a good, story-based summary will indicate, in the first paragraph, the specific and differentiated value the person offers. It should then tell their 'backstory,' showing key career or life turning points, including conflicts that moved them forward. Our approach is to help people find key themes that reveal their character while driving their story forward—much like a screenplay—and then end with a 'climactic' paragraph that shows their aspiration for continuing to make a difference in the world."

Traci Maddox and Richard Fuhr are believers. Check out how they transformed their formerly bland third-person profiles into more lively, interesting, and engaging versions.

While many would think the "before" sample below is fine as is, notice how much more engrossing the "after" sample is with the addition of stories, personality, and humor. Take advantage of the opportunity to be creative and have fun (keeping in mind your target audience) with your summary.

## Sample Before and After LinkedIn Summaries

### Traci Maddox

Before headline:

*President and Founder at Sage Peak Associates, Inc.*

Before summary:

*Author & Speaker, Certified Professional Co-Active Coach, and seasoned program manager with extensive experience in implementing change in both large and small organizations, as well as strategic planning, coaching, and team leadership. Skilled in various change management methodologies, including Kotter and ADKAR. Primary strength is a holistic approach; providing top quality products and services to clients while furthering organizational goals and keeping within cost, schedule, and performance requirements. Recently published* The Essential Employee, *a book about five key employee behaviors in the workplace.*

**Traci Maddox**

After headline:

*Executive Coach, Author, and Organization Development Consultant*

After summary:

*I am an adventurer. Whether I'm bicycling across North America or finding a new way to help an organization be more effective, I want to create an experience that brings people alive! If you want to have fun while learning and growing, I'm the right person for you.*

*I started my career as a computer scientist back in the day when personal computers were new and exciting! While I loved using my technical background to work with a team and create new technology products, I quickly found that my passion was the team, not the technology.*

*Throughout my federal career, I loved the big picture and strategy components of what I did and gravitated toward those kinds of jobs. First, that led me to program management—big, complex systems with people as the backbone. Once I was a program manager, I led large and small teams, and found I loved motivating people and leading them to their best performance. This, I realized, was my true passion and would be my legacy.*

*So I pursued my passion and went back to school for Organization Development, using my work for practical applications of my new training. I moved into the Corporate Business Office and created structures for organizational success—linked, of course, by the people who are critical to the success of any change.*

*I started my own business in 2002 and found my true calling: helping people and organizations reach their peak! Along the way, I achieved my certification in Co-Active coaching and use that training and all my accumulated experience to coach executives and facilitate groups.*

*My newest adventure is that of author and speaker. My first book is based on research, but is written as a novel. It's about the five key behaviors you must have to be considered essential in the workplace.* The Essential Employee *is my vehicle to help all entry-level employees—even those I can't connect with personally—reach their peak.*

*What's the next adventure? I'm excited to find out!*

**Richard Fuhr**

Before headline:

*Director of Professional Services*

Before summary:

*Open to relocation.*

*An energetic, results-driven leader with extensive experience in managing all aspects of a Professional Services organization. Proven ability to build effective working relationships with sales teams, prospects, customers, the business and technology communities, direct reports, senior executives, partners and 3rd-party vendors. Successful track record of consistently growing team revenue and margin.*

*Possesses additional expertise in the following areas:*

- *Proposal Development*
- *Contract Negotiation*
- *Process Improvement*
- *Strategic Planning*
- *Team Building*
- *Creative Problem Solving*

*Six Sigma, Black Belt Training completed*

*Project Management Institute, Project Management Professional (PMP) Certification*

*Fluent in English and French, with dual USA / French Nationalities*

**Richard Fuhr**

After headline:

*Director of Professional Services*

After summary:

*I am a competitor who expects a lot from others and even more from myself. No stranger to demanding and complex situations, my proudest moments are leading teams to challenging destinations. I have successfully delivered projects in ten countries and built multiple organizations from the ground up.*

*As a professional services (PS) leader, I bring creativity, calculated risk taking, the ability to create appropriate structure, and an international perspective to achieving results. My talent in building strong relationships is key to my success.*

*After my MBA, I moved to Paris with my future wife. It was a wonderful cultural exposure that also allowed me to gain hands-on experience in Marketing for a multinational. My perspective broadened when I took on a project management role installing station platform doors for the Hong Kong Metro.*

*It was a pivotal experience that showed me the importance of tying together business, technology, and high performing teams to produce extraordinary results. It also led to being recruited as a business and technology consultant serving clients throughout Europe.*

*When I returned to the States, I took on management roles at two software vendors. At each, I was accountable for growing the PS team, leading process improvements, and actively securing and overseeing client engagements. I enjoyed my work, yet took advantage of an offered opportunity to build a metrics and project estimation unit and then perform internet marketing for a major insurance company. While the work was interesting and I enjoyed meeting objectives, I realized my passion was in leading PS organizations and decided to return.*

*I aspire to launch, grow, and lead PS teams to exceptional levels of achievement. I look forward to providing my team members with personal and professional growth they will cherish the rest of their lives. I am also driven to build loyal and delighted customers who say they have never had technology implementations completed so effortlessly.*

Can you see how using first-person voice and peppering stories throughout the summary can provide an authentic glimpse into their personalities and character? These profiles leap off the screen and make readers eager to learn more!

# Create Your Story

To help add a bit of personality to your LinkedIn profile, complete the following statements and weave your responses into a story.

*When managers/clients/friends speak of me favorably, they call me* ___
_____
_____

*The one time in my career that I felt truly alive was when I was* _____
_____

*My dream job would be* _____
_____

*If I had to compare myself to a major appliance, I'd be a [please explain why]* _____
_____

*My favorite job was [please explain why]* _____
_____

*I place a high value on* _____
_____

*I am adept at* _____
_____

*Some of my specialties/areas of expertise include* _____
_____

*What ultimately makes me unique is* _____
_____

*Once, there was a time when I was doing something I really loved and I did it really well [tell a story of when you saved the day, solved the problem, or served the client]* _____

_____

## Asking for a Connection

When attempting to connect with someone on LinkedIn, you'll be offered a default message: "I'd like to add you to my professional network." Stop. Do not pass Go. Delete it immediately and write a personal message about why you want to connect with this person. Customizing your request will greatly increase the chance that recipients will accept your invitation.

Rabbi R. Karpov, PhD, a career strategist with Résumé Clarity, urges job seekers to let appreciation come from the heart—to be thoughtful when thanking those who have helped them along the way and to do so with more than a simple "thank you." Here are just a few of her suggestions:

- **Acknowledge the new contact by name (and title as applicable), such as:**

*Dear Dr. Brown*

- **Acknowledge something in his or her background.**
  For those in vital but underpaid service industries:

*Thanks for what you do—especially the parts that you think nobody sees.*

For those in life-saving industries, such as medical or radiological technicians:

*Thank you for the lives you've touched and saved.*

- **If you haven't met him or her in person, you could add:**

*Though we have not yet met in person, I hope it is only a matter of time!*

- **Acknowledge the contact's contribution to your life, and share how you have learned from him or her:**

*I appreciate having learned from you about _____, including indirectly through our [mutual, several, (list number of mutual connections, if there are many)] colleagues.*

Often you will be able to make a more personal connection based on a mutual interest, hobby, or shared mission:

- *I see you are on the membership committee for the Cornell University alumni association here in D.C. You've been doing great things!*
- *I am the founder of a nonprofit coaching/consulting firm in Northern Virginia and would like to make your acquaintance due to our LinkedIn Group Association interests. I believe that we might have some synergies between our businesses.*
- *Although we haven't yet met in person, I appreciate learning about you from your profile and indirectly through our 10 connections. I would be honored to be added to your LinkedIn network.*

Or, if you know the person, your request can go something like this:

*Hi, Josh—It's been so long! I hope you remember me. You worked in marketing at AOL while I was in sales. Are you still running marathons? I'm working on expanding my network and would be so honored if you'd accept this invitation to reconnect.*

Convinced yet? As you can see from the examples above, these types of invitations are much more engaging than the standard LinkedIn default messages and will help propel your search forward.

## Following Up

Once people start accepting your invitations to connect, call them. If that makes you queasy, email them. Be friendly, nice, and curious! Ask questions. Don't worry what people will think or feel strange about connecting. People want to help you, if you can get out of your own way and let them do it. LinkedIn's purpose is not just to expand your network; it's to network with your network! So, once a contact accepts your request, follow up with a phone call or email.

### Sample Follow-Up Emails After an Accepted Connection Request

Thank you so much for connecting with me! I look forward to discovering how I may be able to help grow your network and achieve your goals. Would you be willing to meet for coffee [if the contact is local] or chat briefly via phone for a few minutes at your convenience?

## MORE REQUESTS TO CONNECT

We really liked these examples from Kathy Bernard, a career and corporate communicator with GetaJobTips.com:

- *I read your blog regularly and love your advice.* (Believe me, bloggers never tire of such messages!)
- *You may recall that I met you at the networking event. I was the person who was very impressed with your business card.*
- *I see you also worked at XYZ Corp. I'd like to invite you to connect.*
- *I see that you are also an alum of the University of Missouri. Go Tigers!*
- Similarly, you could send messages to your particular school: *I see you were a 1995 Business School grad, too. I bet we had Econ 101 together. I'd like to invite you to connect.*
- You could also invite people from your fraternity or sorority, even from a different college, saying something like: *I see you are a Kappa Kappa Gamma from ABC University. I was one at the University of XYZ.*
- *I've enjoyed reading your comments on the* [group name] *discussion board. I think we share a lot of the same perspectives.*
- *I know we have not yet met, but my friend Susie Smith speaks so highly of you, I wanted to invite you to connect to introduce myself.*
- *I heard you speak at an event and was so inspired by your message.*
- *I've seen you in the XYZ Co. Cafeteria, but have not yet had the opportunity to introduce myself.*

*continued from page 119*

> • *I'm a fellow St. Louisian and noticed that we have 34 mutual connections, so I thought I would invite you to connect in case our knowing each other might be mutually beneficial.*

Or try this message, which works like a charm for Bob McIntosh, a career trainer in Boston:

Thank you for accepting my invitation to be part of my network. I know we can be of mutual assistance to each other! As you'll note from my LinkedIn profile, I am a [your occupation] with a great interest in [your mission]. I'd like to know about you and how we can assist each other in [business or career]. Feel free to contact me at any time via email or my cell phone at [number]. I'd like to grow our new relationship.

Sometimes, Bob says, a simple thank you is all the doctor ordered:

Great to connect with you on LinkedIn. Thanks for accepting my request to connect. I look forward to chatting with you and helping in any way I can. Have a great week!

## How Is InMail Different?

If you don't have a first- or second-degree connection to someone on LinkedIn or an email address for that person, communicating directly can be a challenge. LinkedIn's InMail feature enables you to send a message directly to another LinkedIn member without involving other connections. This feature is currently available to paid members of LinkedIn with available InMail credits. If you're using a free account, you have to pay for individual InMail credits to reach other members through InMail.

This service is basically a private message that enables you to reach other members, but it protects those members' privacy and email addresses. If the person you are writing to accepts the message, you'll receive a notification in your LinkedIn inbox with the other party's name and email address, and you can communicate further. In some cases, you see only the other person's professional headline first, and then you see the person's name after he accepts your InMail message.

Keep your message focused on why you would like to talk to this person, and/or what information you were hoping to exchange.

### Sample InMail from a Job Seeker to a Local Contact (Whom He Does Not Know)

*Dear [contact name],*

*I am hoping that we may network, as I am currently trying to identify a few companies that may be a fit for me in the D.C.-metro area, and was thrilled to find you here. I graduated from the School of Labor and Industrial Relations and Human Resources Management at Michigan State University just one year ago. I recently moved to the D.C. area and intend to ramp up my job-search efforts.*

*With your exciting background in labor law, I was thinking that you may know about firms and/or companies that hire qualified people with experience in labor relations. I'd love to have an opportunity to speak with you about your work and get your feedback on the landscape of labor law in D.C. Would you be open to a quick call to chat? I appreciate your time and consideration!*

*Sincerely,*

*[Your name]*

## Status Updates

The LinkedIn status is one of several ways you can engage your connections, by:

- Keeping your name in front of your connections (any time you update your status, you show up in your contacts' news feed).

- Letting your connections know what you are doing (staying top of mind).
- Adding value to your network by sharing things they may be interested in (showcasing your competence in your chosen field).

There are endless ways to leverage your LinkedIn status updates to connect and communicate with your network. For instance, you may share updates about:

1. **What you are doing professionally that may be relevant to your network:**
   *Attending a local SHRM chapter meeting today and looking forward to hearing a presentation on Social Media and the HR Executive*

2. **Something mentioned within your network that you find newsworthy:**
   *Great post from [colleague name] on the importance of resumes for blue-collar jobs. What are your thoughts? [link]*

3. **An inspiring blog post, cutting-edge web tool, or unique upcoming webinar:**
   *Terrific web tool for marketing whiz kids . . . [link].*

## ⇨ CAREER SUCCESS TIP

A note of caution about status updates: Do not confuse LinkedIn with Facebook; there is no posting of family pictures or rambling on about the good ol' college days here. This is a business networking site. If you are a manager in manufacturing, your updates should be, for the most part, about the manufacturing industry. You can source content from places such as technorati.com and alltop.com and by reading trade journals and/or the blogs of industry insiders if you are having difficulty coming up with details to share.

### Status Updates When Employed

Brenda Bernstein of TheEssayCoach suggests the following for employed users of LinkedIn who fear intrusion of privacy on the site.

"Never fear! The good news is that recruiters do not just browse the profiles of the unemployed. They have a time-honored tradition of finding not-completely-happily-employed people and enticing them to move elsewhere! So, keep your status bar updated with interesting business news that will catch potential clients' attention, or use it to let your boss know what a great job you are doing! You will by default catch recruiters' attention as they search through LinkedIn, and the boss never has to know."

### Status Updates When Unemployed

Brenda has some great advice for keeping your language positive and engaging when you are unemployed. Note: You do NOT have to say anything in your status about looking for work. If you just attended a conference, or if you are studying the latest trends in your field, share that instead. But if you are looking for employment inquiries, here's what NOT to say:

*... is enjoying acting in her first theatrical production!* (Why would you have this update posted for 12 days? What about your job search?)

*... is looking for a job in IT.* (This is boring and too broad.)

*... Any help would be appreciated.* (Desperate?)

*... 1 month ago.* (Update, please?)

*... 3 months ago.* (Really. Update. Please?)

Some better updates:

*... is ravenously reading up on healthcare-reform debate and stimulus-package issues.*

Karen Siwak, executive and principal consultant for Resume Confidential, advises job seekers to reply with the following template when approached (or confronted, as is often the case) by a boss who is alerted to an employee's LinkedIn changes:

*I received an invitation to connect on LinkedIn from [big client (or potential big client)] and realized that it's been a while since I had a look at my profile. Frankly, it was skimpy. Our clients see this page, and I wanted to create a stronger impression of what we do.*

or

*Following [name of an event] I went to last week, I got a lot of new invites to connect, and wanted to present a more up-to-date profile of our company.*

or

*As an active member of [association], I was advised to update my profile so that other members can connect with me.*

---

This job seeker shows anyone who's looking that she is keeping up-to-date on current issues in her field, which helps make her marketable.

*. . . is seeking full-time employment as an H.R. manager in the Boston area.*

If your headline is strong, this update will be a nice complement and will present itself as an opportunity for recruiters!

*. . . is actively networking and researching opportunities with established and growing architecture practices.*

[This one shows you are doing your part to create a great position for yourself, without looking like you need help or are desperate for work.]

Brenda notes, "Neglected LinkedIn profiles get less eyeballs and attention, so consider how often you post to your LinkedIn profile carefully. One posting every few days is a good idea, and won't take more than three to five minutes of your time to execute."

# Commenting on Others' Status Updates

If one of your connections does something you believe your network would benefit from, share it or comment on it.

## ⤷ CAREER SUCCESS TIP

Get into the habit of logging onto LinkedIn in the morning—at least a few times a week. Move your cursor over All Updates and select the Recent view to see the complete list of updates (a.k.a. news feeds) via the home page. By browsing these updates, you can easily glean what people are discussing and uncover what your contacts are up to. In addition, you can elect to receive a weekly email from updates@LinkedIn.com entitled "LinkedIn Network Updates," featuring various changes reflected in your connections' profiles.

These weekly digests contain key source material for future conversations: Profile Changes (often includes promotions, new titles, company moves), Posts (with links to relevant articles and/or blog posts), New Connections, and Jobs You May Be Interested In. Open these emails and take note of any key changes to those in your network. If you see company moves or new job titles, jot them down; later you will want to comment on their status to nurture relationships with these contacts.

Quick comments on another status could look like:

*Great link to the article on Malcolm Gladwell's books . . . have you read them all? I'm a huge fan too.*

*Interesting read. It needed to be said. Really have to keep an eye on these events for our friends and contacts. Great reminder!*

# Searching in Status Updates

Recruiters can search your status updates, too. Simply entering keywords related to the job they are trying to fill will yield interesting results about what folks are sharing, in real time, on any given topic. (To search, go to the drop-down box in the upper right-hand corner and select Updates, just below People.) Of course, this too is a terrific way to search for job postings. For example, {"hiring" + "manufacturing"} yielded 304 updates of folks in our network, and served up a list of status updates from users who have posted about jobs in manufacturing.

Make your status updates keyword-rich to attract more employer eyeballs.

*IBM Acquisition of Emptoris bolsters Smarter Commerce Initiative and helps reduce procurement costs and risks.* (Searched on "procurement.")

*Three Tips for Boosting Productivity with Project Debriefing* (Searched on "project management.")

*9 Ways to Measure Your Inbound Marketing ROI.* (Searched on "marketing.")

*Manufacturing jobs are up this year! [link to article]* (Searched on "manufacturing.")

*Pam Parsons, who led design/construction group at Host Hotels & Resorts, joins Forrest Perkins in Washington DC as VP of Ops.* (Searched on "construction.")

# Communicating via Answers

LinkedIn Answers is a great forum to share business knowledge. In it, you can:

- Showcase your knowledge, expertise, and interests by answering questions. (Widely considered to be the best reason to use the Answers feature.)
- Ask your question and get fast, accurate answers from your network and other experts worldwide.
- Stay up-to-date on the latest opinions from those in your industry and functional area.

When considering categories in which to answer questions, Dorothy Tannahill Moran, career coach with Next Chapter New Life Coaching, suggests asking yourself one question: "Historically, what is it that people have sought me out for? For example, are you conducting a job search in marketing, but all of your expertise has been in healthcare? You would be primed to search the healthcare industry for marketing jobs (and answering questions pertaining to both categories can only help you do that!). If you can offer a unique perspective and help another LinkedIn user by addressing a problem or offering a solution, Answers is your platform."

Ready to submit a question or answer one? One quick search of LinkedIn Answers yields all the possibilities you need. While you are free to answer in any category you choose, strategically it's best to limit your replies to your major areas of expertise (albeit functional or industry) and/or a job-search inquiry.

## Example of Job-Search-Related Q&A

While in a job search, you may elect to ask *and/or* answer questions, like these below, to get fast answers from your network, showcase your expertise, and stay up-to-date on the latest opinions from those in your industry or functional area.

**Q:** *What's your advice for a for-profit professional interviewing at a nonprofit organization?* (Note: This is a good question to ask if you are in an open job search.)

**A:** *My experience with both for-profits and not-for-profits aligns with Patricia's comments. It is definitely not about making a profit; it's about improving capacity at all levels . . . with achieving the organization's mission, gaining more funding, building the volunteer base, generating more exposure through events, etc. Everyone believes in what they are doing and is excited to be working for an organization that makes a valuable contribution to the community or society.*

### Example of Business Development (Industry) Q&A

**Q:** *Do you focus more on adding new customers or nurturing your current clients?*

**A:** *Creating a customer-loyalty program is the best sales tool and the best way to retain customers. For example, credit cards like those issued by American Express and the banks have offered regular customers a range of valuable benefits. In business-to-business markets, loyal customers have traditionally been treated better than those who buy "on the spot." In recent years, loyalty schemes have attracted considerable interest as a wider range of companies practice one of marketing's most familiar strategies, namely, "if you see a good idea—copy it."*

## Communicating with Value via LinkedIn Groups

LinkedIn Groups comprises online communities of professionals who have common interests, affiliations, professions, or goals. There are groups focused on industry affiliations or professions. There are groups for alumni of colleges and universities, and there are groups for start-up small businesses. There are literally thousands and thousands of groups covering every industry or interest. For example, if you are a purchasing procurement leader, you could join the Procurement Professionals group, with 30,000 members, or Supply Chain Today, which has 15,000 participants.

What happens after you join a LinkedIn group? You'll have access to the group's information, activities, and members. There are many benefits to your job search. You will/can:

- Network with others in your specific field, and ultimately expand your LinkedIn network.
- Expose yourself to articles and industry best practices to help keep your skills current.
- Participate in industry discussions and demonstrate your skills, abilities, and knowledge.
- Search group members to identify other members who work for, or used to work for, your target company, and who may be able to provide important inside information about the company.
- Have the ability to directly email other members, and they can do the same to you. Review statistics about groups to decide which ones to join.

Communicating via groups requires careful consideration. These updates have a long shelf life (depending on the group user's communication preferences) and are often emailed directly to hundreds (if not thousands) of users' inboxes daily. Avoid quick, thoughtless comments.

A discussion of groups would not be complete without sharing what NOT to do.

LinkedIn Groups is not the place for:

- **Derogatory communication** (we were particularly outraged when we read this one):
  *Subject: Don't lend any money to [person's name]. I used to work at [Company X] from 2004 to 2007. [Name] came to me for $3,700 to help her daughter get a truck that was impounded. The truck got*

*destroyed soon thereafter and I've been struggling to get my money back ever since! She's bad news despite being an executive secretary!*

Whoa! Way to ruin two reputations at once.

- **Constant self-promotion:** LinkedIn users can overlook someone who advertises goods and services (even though LinkedIn—the company—frowns on it) on an infrequent basis IF the user is a frequent and generous communicator in that group. But be cautious of how many posts you write of this nature, because group owners (and LinkedIn in general) can suspend users who disregard this rule.
- **Begging for a job:** The group is not there to get you hired; however, if you have a specific question about your job search, LinkedIn Groups is the perfect outlet.

Alternatively, consider employing the following six proven LinkedIn Groups job-search tactics:

1. **Introduce yourself:**
   *Hi, all. I'm new to DC Connections and I'd like to introduce myself. I'm a marketing consultant with a passion for, and expertise in, the real-estate industry. If you need a great realtor, I know quite a few!*

2. **Post a job description on behalf of a recruiter, friend, or colleague. (Spread the wealth on jobs for which you are not a fit):**
   *A friend is looking to fill a systems-analyst position in McLean, VA. Send your resume to [email], if interested.*

3. **Write a book review on a topic specific to your industry or expertise, and consider listing it as a book you've read via the Amazon application:**
   *Reviewed: William Horton's thorough, practical guide to creating excellent eLearning. Published in October of this year, this book is an update to William Horton's 2006 book. Horton reorganized the content and added excellent sections on games, social*

*networking, and mobile technology. This is a book that belongs in your library.*

**4. Share a challenge you are facing at your company (if employed)—or an industry challenge—and request feedback:** *My company is two months away from an acquisition of another multi-branded restaurant company. Does anyone have any change-management workshop materials they can share? Executive briefings?*

**5. Announce a program, seminar, workshop, or relevant professional development opportunity. You can also post these using the Events application:** *ASTD Atlanta: Talent Management for Workplace Learning Professionals Webinar Series. Greater Atlanta ASTD is taking professional development to a higher level! It is a pleasure to announce a new and exciting initiative for 2012: Talent Management for Workplace Learning Professionals.*

**6. Seek out a job-search buddy:** *Subject: Seeking accountability partner. It's true that the Five O'Clock Clubbers are getting jobs faster, and my previous accountability partner is one of them! Now I'm on the lookout for another job-hunting buddy, but I'm only looking for someone who is serious about the methodology.*

## Career Success Steps

Peruse the headlines of others in your industry and find a format that is appealing to you, then craft a defining sentence that has some "zing." Remember to first identify your target audience and consider the value you provide. Next, pepper your headline with any relevant keywords (if they add credibility). Finally, make it memorable. No "blah" headlines here!

If you are on LinkedIn already, boost your profile to 100% complete. Then give it a good once-over and consider giving your summary an extreme makeover. Infuse it with authentic stories that help you cross the bridge to the employer and make you more approachable and personable.

When adding connections, customize your default with a quick note about who you are and why you wish to connect; customizing your message will greatly increase the chance that recipients will accept your invitation.

After a connection has been accepted, follow up with a phone call or email. Nurture the relationship: be friendly and interested; ask questions. And if it makes sense, suggest a phone meeting to discuss synergies.

Create a week's worth of status updates and set yourself a daily reminder to post them to your profile. As we discussed, your status is one of several ways you can engage your connections, so keep your name in front of them, let them know what you are doing, and add value to your network by sharing things they may find interesting (while showing your competence in your chosen field).

Comment on others' status updates. Get into the habit of logging onto LinkedIn in the morning and scrolling through the All Updates section (a.k.a. news feed) via the home page. By browsing these updates, you can easily glean what people are discussing and uncover what your contacts are up to. Open these emails and take note of any key changes to those in your network. If you see company moves or new job titles, comment on the status updates to nurture your relationships with these contacts.

Start a Q&A campaign by searching through Answers categories in which you can demonstrate your expertise, and leap in with either a question or a well-thought-out answer.

Communicate within Groups. To interact with your fellow group members, use any of the following tactics:

- Post a job description on behalf of a recruiter, friend, or colleague.
- Write a book review on a topic specific to your industry or expertise.

- Share a challenge you are facing at your company (if employed)—or an industry challenge—and request feedback.
- Announce a program, seminar, workshop, or relevant professional development opportunity.
- Seek out a job-search buddy.

Remember, don't beg for a job or be overly solicitous. LinkedIn Groups are not the place for this type of communication.

Regardless of the amount of time you spend on LinkedIn, don't mistake your reasons for using the tool: to cultivate the relationships you make and to take many of them offline. Don't rely on "drive-by" updates (logging on, posting an update, and logging off), as there is so much more to do with this essential job-search networking tool; so sit down and stay awhile. Take time to send an email to your contacts, pick up the phone, or offer to meet for coffee. Go for quality over quantity with your connections, and you'll have more than enough in no time.

# 12 Communicating Professionally Using Twitter

**Y**ou've probably seen references to Twitter on television or in magazines, even if you have never used it yourself. This social network allows users to communicate publicly by posting messages that are 140 characters or fewer. (The two sentences you just read have 225 characters; tweets are very short.) Don't let the platform's required brevity trick you into overlooking its value. If you think Twitter is trivial, or if you believe it exists to allow you to broadcast uninteresting details about your life, think again!

## Why Use Twitter?

Twitter is a terrific network to help you interact with others online. It fits perfectly into the framework outlined in Chapter 10.

- **Learn what thought leaders in your industry are thinking and writing about.** You may be surprised to learn that

Twitter is not just for paparazzi and public relations professionals. For example, a MediaBistro.com article endorsed Twitter as the number one social network for financial-services companies. It cites a *Financial Times* report indicating that Twitter's popularity is rising among financial groups, with an increase in Twitter use from 57% to 66% in less than one year. The article quotes Alan Maginn, senior analyst at Corporate Insight, who believes Twitter is more popular for financial businesses because of its focus on content: "In our opinion . . . Twitter is more content-driven. With Twitter, they can concentrate more on the value of the content they produce."

Once you recognize Twitter as a resource and critical information source, you can learn to collect and share professional data and details to help fuel your job hunt. If you are unemployed or are a career changer, Twitter can help you keep your finger on the pulse of your industry or target field.

- **Meet new people and expand your network.** On Twitter, you do not need an introduction to interact and engage with people from all over the world. You can simply identify whom you'd like to meet and tweet a question, retweet (forward) someone else's tweet (what they shared), or just jump into a conversation in real-time. It is easy to get to know your mentors and leaders in your field via Twitter and to meet other people just like you—professionals who want to share information about your mutual interests.

  Meeting colleagues via Twitter can be as easy as finding and following a hashtag (a search term, designated by a # sign; for example, #healthcareers), so that you can keep track of conversations. Once you identify people tweeting interesting information, you'll be able to use the advice in this chapter to interact with them.

# "I EXPANDED MY NETWORK VIA TWITTER"

Rachel Sweeney is a senior at Marist College. She twice interned at Burberry, loves accessories design, and is majoring in fashion merchandising. She explains:

"I was slow to take to the Twitter trend; tweeting about what I do all day long—could anything be more narcissistic? Then I caved. Actually, I more than caved; I am slightly obsessed. I have to admit I do follow a handful of silly tweeters that help put a giggle or two in my day, but on the whole, I use Twitter to keep me up to speed on all things current in my related industry. Fashion is my realm of interest, and Twitter has helped me get even more connected.

"I use my account to keep up on current information and advance my knowledge, whether it be a news post on the latest detail from the *New York Times* or the hottest trending jacket silhouette in street style.

"For example, I follow these people and companies:

**Fashion bloggers:** @Stylescrapbook, @Refinery29, and @Chictopia.

**Companies:** @Burberry and @Gucci.

**Other contacts:** @StyleCaster, @AP_Fashion (Associated Press), @CFDA (the Council of Fashion Designers), and @Styledotcom.

"Would you really want to step into an interview and answer no when they ask if you follow their company on Twitter? They probably would not take you as seriously.

Following target companies is a great way to get information straight from the source, and quickly. Following news sources, industry leaders, and noteworthy tweeters has put me one step closer to getting a job. Twitter allows me to network with people I thought would be out of my reach. Recently, I reached out to Sasha Charnin Morrison, a past contributor to *Allure*, *Elle*, and *Vanity Fair*. She is currently the fashion director at *US Weekly*, and she responded! These were our exchanges:

It was great meeting you @sashacharnin! I completely enjoyed your book signing; thank you for spending your time with us!

@IndieTwenty_RS my absolute pleasure and great meeting you!

@sashacharnin If possible, like I mentioned, Marist would love for you to come speak to us. Please let me know!

@IndieTwenty_RS that would be awesome!

@sashacharnin Fantastic! Rachel.Sweeney1@Marist.edu is my email for your convenience; if another form of contact is easier please let me know

"Getting an answer from such an influential person put in perspective how valuable a tool Twitter is if you use it right. I tweet at companies, use hashtags, and retweet to get noticed. It is exciting to accrue new followers who find me, especially those who have 67,000 followers of their own."

## Rachel's Sample Tweets

@voguemagazine I cannot wait to get my hands on the special edition of #VogueBestDressed! vogue.com/vogue-daily/ar . . . @EmeryKnapp let's get it!

Check it style lovers: http://www.ilovemeagan.com/#/fashionii and: http://www.chictopia.com/ Thanks for the follows @MeaganCignoli and @chictopia!

Tom Ford eyed for @HM's next designer collaboration http://nym.ag/rzIzF5

#MSNBC's Chris Matthews fielded questions about his new book, "Jack Kennedy: Elusive Hero." #CNFashion #Womensweardaily wwd.com/media-news/fas...

- **Demonstrate your expertise.** If you are an expert in your field but no one knows it yet, it will be difficult to advance your online brand, which goes hand in hand with your career. When you become a trusted resource providing information, opinions, and expertise to your colleagues (or prospective colleagues), you will increase the number of people who know, like, and trust you exponentially.
- **Be found.** Connecting with people and sharing information via tweets will make it easier for people who are looking for someone like you . . . to find you! You may be surprised by how easy it can be to connect with someone when you hit exactly the right nerve.

# A SUCCESS STORY: USING TWITTER TO CONNECT WITH DECISION-MAKERS (AND MAYBE LAND A JOB!)

Hanna Phan is a product manager at SlideRocket, a presentation platform that brings ideas to life. Prior to joining SlideRocket, Hanna was a business communication consultant specializing in presentation design for high-tech and nonprofit companies. She explains, "After searching on and off for a full-time position for over a year, I'd had it up to here with job hunting . . . Finally, I came to this realization: I didn't want to be just another corporate drone. But if that was the case, it was imperative that I continue my job search with a completely different approach." Narrowing down her target companies, she determined she'd like to combine her management and creative problem-solving skills to work for a company that built a presentation application. (Talk about specific!)

Hanna identified SlideRocket and decided it was a perfect match. She considered options to catch the employer's eye and determined, "Considering that SlideRocket was a presentation company, it was obvious that I needed to make a presentation about myself, rather than going through the traditional H.R. portal. Creating a Présumé (presentation + résumé) with SlideRocket's own software would not only showcase my presentation/creative skills; it would illustrate my love of the product itself."

Noting that Chuck Dietrich, CEO of SlideRocket, was quite active on Twitter, she used her Présumé as a hook, and tweeted her presentation link directly to him. (View Hanna's Présumé via a link on our website: 100ConversationsForCareerSuccess.com.)

> @chuckdietrich @sliderocket I want to work with you! Find my application here: http://bit.ly/yjlS3G

An hour later, after Chuck literally walked off a plane, he replied:

> @hannaphan @sliderocket AMAZING Preso! Let's talk.

She explains the happy ending: "No sooner than Chuck tweeted me back, I was on the phone with the company's C.M.O. SlideRocket even featured my Présumé in their Inspiration Gallery and newsletter. I flew to San Francisco for a round of interviews—and the rest is history. I had finally landed my dream job—not by going the traditional H.R. route,

continued from page 139

but with careful thought and the guts to do something radically different to rise above the crowd."

Chuck Dietrich explains why Hanna's materials stood out: "It was an engaging story about her and more importantly why she wanted to be a part of the SlideRocket team. Her Présumé allowed her to showcase her uniqueness and garner the attention that she deserved." He was also impressed with the way she reached out via Twitter and said her methodology was ". . . indicative of a successful entrepreneur. Employers are always looking for employees who think and act like entrepreneurs by finding savvy ways to achieve results."

## TWITTER NETWORKING CONTACTS CAN MAKE A DIFFERENCE

Deborah Jacobs wrote an article for *Forbes* highlighting another Twitter success story. Joshua Filgate, a 27-year-old engineer in Massachusetts, had lost his job after more than four years at the company. Jacobs noted, "He updated his resume and his LinkedIn profile, applied for 100 positions listed on Internet job sites, and let family, friends, and former co-workers know he was out of work. Within a week, one contact (a venture capitalist in the Boston area) sent him a text message with the name of another venture capitalist who he recommended Joshua follow on Twitter (neither of whom knew the VC personally).

"Even though he had never used Twitter, Joshua signed up. Coincidentally, not long after following the venture capitalist (a partner at the Boston firm General Catalyst), the contact tweeted:

What are top recruitment firms for mechanical engineers, process engineers, materials scientists, manufacturing engineers?

The *Forbes* piece notes:

"Filgate replied: Funny that you ask . . . If it's an engineer you seek, you should dm me."

The article goes on to explain how the two moved the conversation to email: "The VC suggested Joshua submit his resume to the human resources department of ARC-Energy, a Nashua, NH-based clean-tech startup, and copy him on the e-mail." While he had already applied there and had not heard anything, the networking contact helped him land an interview—and a job!

# How to Brand Yourself on Twitter

### Your Twitter Bio

Your Twitter bio should make it easy for people to know what you do and how you can help them. Remember, as with any job-search communication, the easiest way to create an appealing bio is to first identify the skills, experiences, and accomplishments your employers value and then demonstrate that you are a strong match for their needs.

## ⮑ CAREER SUCCESS TIP

Hubspot's research shows Twitter users with a bio have on average more than eight times more followers than those who do not. Additionally, Twitter profiles including a link to their website or LinkedIn profile have more than seven and a half times the followers than those with no link.

When your optimized LinkedIn profile is complete, you can repurpose the content in your Twitter bio. (See Chapter 11 for examples of effective LinkedIn headlines.) Don't use the exact same verbiage if you can help it, but borrowing a few perfect keywords is fine by us!

Twitter allows you 160 characters (letters and spaces) to use in your bio, so select every letter wisely. While it is fun to incorporate aspects of your personality, limit non-keyword content until you incorporate the most important details. For example, if you are a "fun mom," "soccer dad," "love Looney Tunes," or "Are the #1 Braves fan," you may opt to leave those details out until you are certain you have enough room for your content-rich information. Additionally, unless they are related to your profession, it is generally wise to leave out references to religion and politics. Focus on what is special about you and how you solve problems, and avoid vague or nonspecific language or information.

Jorgen Sundberg, social-recruiting and online-branding consultant at Link Humans in London, suggests getting directly to the point and incorporating the following structure in your Twitter bio:

1. **Be specific.** Start with: *I provide banks with insurance solutions* or *I help people achieve fitness through pilates.* Make sure you include your relevant keywords so you will appear in search results. List any product or service names you expect potential customers to enter in search boxes.
2. **List a few specialties that set your personal brand apart:** *First certified scuba instructor in Greenland* or *Passionate about your customer experience.* You can also include any notable achievements or people you are associated with, such as: *Author of the best-selling book* Twitterati; *Previous owner of the Springfield Isotopes;* or *Special advisor to Henry Kissinger.*
3. **End it with a call to action, a statement, or a question.** For example: *Contact me for details.*

## TWITTER-BIO MAKEOVER

Marian Schembari is a blogger, traveler, and all-around social media thug. She's based in Auckland, New Zealand, hails from Connecticut, and blogs at marianlibrarian.com. She dissected the following Twitter bio in a post for Brazen Life, a lifestyle and career blog for ambitious young professionals hosted by Brazen Careerist. Take a look at this Twitter bio, and Marian's suggested revisions:

"Recent grad from Fancy College. ~*~*~ HIRE ME ~*~*~ #communications #marketing #health

### No-no: 'Recent grad from Fancy College'

You have 140 characters on Twitter to show off your skills. Do you think anyone will care what college you went to? Maybe, but new graduates often put more emphasis on school than necessary. Your university can provide a great connection; if someone sees you graduated from their alma matter, that could open some doors. Remember—very few

continued from page 142

people you meet on Twitter will have gone to your school. That means maybe your school shouldn't be your number one selling point.

**Instead:** Prioritize your skills, experience, and passion, and add your alma mater only if you have space.

## No-no: 'HIRE ME'

There's something a little desperate about shouting HIRE ME from the social media rooftops. There are other ways to show you're job hunting. Always bring your online behavior back to how you'd act in real life. Would you walk up to someone at your dream company and shout 'HIRE ME!' in their face?

**Instead:** Something as simple as 'Looking for a communications job in Philly' could work. Here are some random examples of ways to mention you are looking for a job without sounding desperate or focusing the reader on you as a job seeker:

*Design-obsessed marketing pro, specializing in bold ad campaigns. Job hunting in New York. My last agency bosses say I'll blow your socks off.*

*Barista in Seattle seeks rad coffee gig. I make a mean flat white. Don't know what a flat white is? Just you wait . . .*

*Perfecting the lost art of the press release while looking for the next big PR job in Chicago. Curious? Read the clips on my website.*

## No-no: ~*~*~

Don't use symbols, starts, or hearts. If you can't think of something better to go there, maybe you need to start again!"

# Sample Twitter Bios

Ultimately, your goal for your Twitter bio is to include information showcasing your professional qualifications. Consider all advice here as a guideline; some of the following examples actually violate Marian's suggestions, but each one incorporates enough data about the person's professional interests and personality to inspire you to click through to learn more.

@jimstroud I train. I speak. I blog a lot. My focus? Social Recruiting and Job search strategy. Let's network.

@stayadventurous Traveled 40states, 40countries & still traveling. Sharing my stories to inspire others to stay adventurous. Founder of #SunsetSunday. Mexico Today Ambassador

@fishdogs Linkedin Certified Training VP - Ajax Social Media • Partner/Recruiter SocialMediaTalent.com • Speaker • Host TalentNet Live Events & #TNL Chat • Dad of 3 boys

@brainzooming Strategy, innovation, creativity, & social media ideas at www.brainzooming.com.

@mnheadhunter Minnesota IT Recruiter I VP Recruiting HireCast Consulting I Blogger I Speaker, Consultant, Trainer: Recruiter, HR, Career & Social Media I Sports & Politics

@maggiemistal CNN dubbed me 1 of the Nation's Best Known Career Coaches. Career Change Expert, Radio Host, and Speaker

@girlmeetsgeek National Journalist and Speaker On Emotional Integrity and Authenticity in Online Media. {Idealist} {Collaborator} {Humanist} {TechAddict} {Photographer}

@phyllismufson Career/business consultant, certified coach, helping people grow - personally and professionally. http://PhyllisMufson.com

@marismith Mari 'like Ferrari!' ≡ Passionate Leader of Social Media, Relationship Marketing & Facebook Mastery. ✈Globetrotting Speaker & Author. ☀Bubbly Scottish-Canadian.

@chinagorman Business leader, public speaker, free agent and supporter of all things HR.

@socialdivo A communication nerd, digital marketer with @engauge & owner of Quarterlife Network, with a passion for connecting people through journalism.

@debra_feldman Strategic Executive Talent Agent guarantees targeted inside contacts|Develops social networks|Accelerates job search results|Creates lifetime career insurance

@davebenjamin One of the original Founders & Social Media Director @SalesBasix eLearning. Joined @thehungrydudes - Foodie! Sometimes sarcastic, always looking to help others.

@berrakdc Writer/Amplifier/Community Mgr @ PQ Productions. VP of Sponsorship

@SMCDC. Co-Organizer for #cmgrDC. Has #PenguinPosse. Loves to meet people for coffee.

## Our Twitter Bios

@Keppie_Careers Job search and social media coach, resume writer & author of Social Networking for Career Success. Empowering successful job seekers & entrepreneurs.

@lauralabovich Job Search Makeover Coach, Award-Winning Resume Writer. Former Disney Recruiter. Extreme Networker! Proud Michigander & Mom to 2 Amazing Kids.

## Sample Job-Seeker Bios

@BethanneEretto I've just moved to St. Augustine, FL looking for entry-level employment in the Jacksonville/St. Augustine area in finance, or non-profit. I'm up for a challenge!

@accanalystbruce Financial Analyst (15+ years) experienced in increasing billings revenue, lowering inventory losses. Seeking new challenges to relocate preferably in NC.

@VickiCorson Marketing and social media junkie; WIT Leadership Awards social media poster; avid blog reader; lifelong learner

# What Types of Accounts to Follow on Twitter—and What to Tweet to Them

Before you can engage in great conversations, strategize about how to find people to follow. Since Twitter is an open network, you do not need to limit yourself to following only people you already know. While there are many Twitter feeds linking to open jobs, you should think of Twitter as a tool to connect with people, not simply as another place to find job listings. Here are some tips to help you search and what to say when you locate ideal contacts:

- **Leaders in your field.** Identify industry experts, potential mentors, and people who are famous in your niche.
  @LeaderInField I can't wait to read your new book. I am hoping to use it with my 9th-grade math students in Salem, MA.
- **Other people who are doing the same job as you, or who tweet about similar interests.**
  @Colleague Looking forward to your reaction to the latest news about _____: [link].
- **Recruiters and human-resources leaders who work in (and tweet about) your industry.** Many recruiters share exactly what they want to hear from job seekers, and they also post opportunities as they arise. Take the chance to learn directly from the horse's mouth.
  @Recruiter I see you have a new posting. I may know someone who is a perfect fit. I will email you the info.
- **Corporate representatives.** Following your target organizations will help you get a feel for the organizations' cultures. If you can create rapport with a company's Twitter representative, you have a much better chance of landing an interview there.
  @Company Thanks for the constant stream of information about the new tax laws. Have you seen this data? [include link]

- **Career coaches.** Many career coaches tweet advice and share links to their own blogs and other information. Identify several who tweet often, and follow them to keep up with what is new in job search.
  @CareerCoach Do you think it's worth looking for a job over the holidays? Isn't everyone on vacation?

- **Professional journals.** Identify if your profession's journal or another reliable news source about your profession has a Twitter feed.
  @ProfessionalJourno Thanks for highlighting the best books of the year for librarians. I appreciated the good read!

- **News organizations.** It's possible to filter all top news via Twitter by following major news sources, including national sources (for example, @CNN or @NYTimes). You may be surprised to find your local newspaper or television news uses Twitter.
  @LocalNews Great coverage of the latest storm damage. Keep up the good work!

- **Your networks.** Consider a variety of networking organizations that may be using Twitter. For example, professional networks, alumni networks, and local/community job clubs.
  @AlumniNetwork I can't believe we made it to the final four! Talk about a Cinderella story! When can alumni buy tickets?

- **Hobbyists.** Don't forget to consider finding and following people who may share your hobbies or personal interests, as long as those hobbies are professional and appropriate for your potential employers to know about.
  @FellowHobbyist What brand of pastels do you use to get those vibrant colors? #artist

# How to Find Specific People on Twitter

Don't forget to snoop around to see who your contacts on Twitter are following, and be sure to check out any public lists your friends or mentors have.

## Have Specific People in Mind to Follow?

Look at their LinkedIn profiles. Often if someone uses Twitter, he or she will share a link on LinkedIn. It's an easy way to connect with your top targets.

If you are using the Twitter client (viewing directly from Twitter .com), take a look at the Activity tab. It shows activity by the people you follow; you will be able to see when they choose a favorite tweet and when they follow new people. It's also a good idea to review the Who to Follow list on the left side of the Twitter client on Twitter.com.

When you visit other people's Twitter profiles, you can also look for their Lists (in the dropdown menu next to the search field). Click through to see if your contacts cultivate lists of people they follow. People usually categorize lists by topic, so it should be easy to find new people to follow who share your interests. Don't hesitate to follow people with common hobbies who tweet about nontraditionally job-related topics.

If you read blogs, bloggers usually showcase a Twitter handle; be sure to follow your favorite bloggers.

In Miriam's book *Social Networking for Career Success*, she recommends these tools:

- http://search.twitter.com/advanced: Twitter's advanced-search tool.
- http://www.twellow.com/: Twellow, the Twitter Yellow Pages.
- http://justtweetit.com/: A directory to help you find other Twitter users.

- http://listorious.com/: Conduct searches using keywords of interest to you; then follow individuals from the lists that result.
- http://wefollow.com/: Search for terms, topics, or people of interest, and follow them.
- http://geofollow.com/: A location-based directory to help you find people.
- http://twibes.com/: Lists to review.
- http://www.followerwonk.com/: Allows you to search bios on Twitter—it's a great tool if you are looking for other people in your field.
- http://www.happn.in/: Find out the most discussed topics in your area.

# How to Get Someone's Attention on Twitter

Setting yourself up with a great bio and finding people to follow and talk to on Twitter are two first steps, but what should you say?

If you are using Twitter to enhance your professional profile, you need to tweet consistently. Broadcasting your ideas, serving as a resource to your target audience, and connecting with new networking contacts requires commitment. Consider tweeting at least two or three times per day.

### Sample Tweets

Ed Cabellon is the director of the Campus Center at Bridgewater State University in Massachusetts. He blogs at http://edcabellon.com/ and tweets @edcabellon. Here are some sample tweets showcasing the major topical areas we suggest you cover:

1. **Content-rich tweets demonstrating your expertise or offering a direct answer to a question.** (This may include links to your own posts or things you wrote.) Ed shares

articles of interest with his colleagues. Note his use of hashtags to attract attention:

Nice post on the @The_SA_Blog by @joeginese: "You've Just Been VolunTold" http://ow.ly/37Tav #sachat #highered

@joeginese Foursquare for Universities is a great place to start: http://ow.ly/36rE6 #sachat Pro Mentors

2. **Retweet news relevant to your field.** Ed posts advice and information about using social media in higher education, indicating he is aware of this issue and connected to people who also write about it:

RT @mikefixs: RT @TweetSmarter: 100 Inspiring Ways to Use #SocialMedia In the Classroom: http://j.mp/9BPH8G #RIT

3. **Let people know if you are speaking or highlighted as an expert.** Ed lets everyone know that he presents about this topic:

Headed over to present to the women of @dphieBSU on Social Media :-) I'm really getting good at this topic ;-) #bsulife

4. **Have direct conversations with potential or existing contacts.** Simply write a brief summary of what you might say in person. If you enjoy reading someone's blog, feel free to use the Twitter stream to say so. Posing a question may encourage a reply. Here's a sample we generated:

@TargetContact I was impressed by your most recent post about leadership lessons. Ever handled #3 yourself? What was the result?

5. **Occasionally, it's okay to share something personal.** For example, if you are a sports fan or enjoy a particular TV show, it's okay to tweet about it. You never know; it's possible to meet a great networking contact via a fun, personal tweet.

@FanOne Can you believe we pulled off that win! Looking forward to the playoffs next week! #GoBears

## *More Sample Tweets*

Laura Schlafly (@LauraSchlafly) is a certified career-management coach and founder of Career Choices with Laura. Her goal is to inspire and guide Baby Boomers to investigate and launch their dream careers after age 50. Here are some of her sample tweets, categorized to show the type of information you can share.

1. **General, inspiration-oriented tweet to catalyze followers:**

   Spark Plug of an Encore Career Coach Catalyzing Boomers to Combine Passion, Purpose, AND a Paycheck. Let's Put Your Pedal to the Metal!

   Be poised to bring new solutions to careers long plagued by outmoded approaches. As #Boomers make the difference.

   #Boomers-instead of freedom from work, R U searching 4 freedom 2 work? Instead of retirement, do you want an #encore career?

2. **Sharing resources and information relevant to her community:**

   AARP survey says more than ½ #boomers who work after retirement feel it is important to help people in their work. http://t.co/xR4RlHHQ

   This is such a powerful article: Andy Rooney's Career Leadership Lesson - Forbes http://onforb.es/s6xb5Q

   Interesting concept of http://socialstrategygroup.com. The rise of the Boomer entrepreneur http://natpo.st/sCfUAb via @financialpost

   #Boomers embarking on an encore career should not assume smooth sailing. Only 12% of adults in a work study think it's easy.

   Studs Terkel in his book "Working" notes that Americans get up & go to work each day as much for daily meaning as for daily bread.

> Hooray for us! RT @usnews: Retiring Baby Boomers Will Change Rules of Hiring - On Retirement (http://usnews.com) http://bit.ly/uoLgDM

3. **Letting followers know about events she's attending:**

> I'll attend 10/28 & 2 meet Marc Freedman in person! http://bit.ly/xyz/

4. **Direct resource targeting her audience:**

> What will you do for your encore career? Tough to change jobs and/or careers after 50. Here's a place to start http://ow.ly/6SvtN

Stephanie True Moss (@truemc and @QRmedia) is founder and chief creative officer of True Moss Communications, Inc. She is author and editor of QRmedia.us and QRmediaGuide.com, a QR-code-services directory. She tweets useful information for people interested in QR code technology. Some samples:

1. **Announcing speaking engagements:**

> Join me for my QR Code presentation today @ Roam in Alpharetta - http://goo.gl/ZSlvl event. #digatl

2. **Useful informational links:**

> Bus Shelter QR Code Unveils Secret Bars | http://goo.gl/jTESr

3. **Specific advice relevant to her field:**

> Eye level, not at the knees! RT @seanbell: @erikg1 ...move the codes to upper right or left of the signs. Too many codes on bottom. #qrchat

> Fun QR code in today's Walmart Toy Catalog. #qrchat http://t.co/imEqPD29

# HOW TO SHARE LINKS
# ON TWITTER WITH IMPACT

Jacqui Barrett-Poindexter, a certified master resume writer and chief career writer and partner with CareerTrend, notes, "Twitter content sharing is about expressing yourself in a unique way while also tending to the needs of people who are following you."

She explains, "Not bound by others' rules in this freeing Twitter social venue, I do feel bound by the message my handle, @ValueIntoWords expresses, as well as my profession in the career writing industry. I am committed to consistently demonstrating that I value the words I use, and exhibiting competent, quality-focused writing abilities.

"I aspire to Tweet links with oomph—creatively and consciously, as well as with a dash of sensitivity. I always read the content before retweeting it. Because I am tweeting links to information, stories, or musings I like, value, respect, and/or want to support, it is natural for me to want to share a tidbit of my takeaway from the article or blog. For example, in a recent Tweet, I said:

> When the going gets tough, do you 'hide under the covers' or push through? bit.ly/vykcM9 by @WorkWithIllness (great 'thinking' post!)

Another link-sharing tweet applied the same strategy:

> (smart post!) Beware of having 'too many' ideas, cut out distractions + other entrepreneurial wisdom fr/ @MsCareerGirl: http://bit.ly/rSgGgT

"The introduction I used in both instances was an amalgamation of language the authors articulated in their posts. I try to lock in on a key phrase or phrases that resonate with me from a post and either directly quote or summarize it in a gently revised way to highlight my personal takeaway. My goal is not to reframe their post, but to authentically share the impact their words had on me in order to draw the reader in for more.

"In other instances, I want to be certain that the post's or article's title is included in the tweet because of its elegant or compelling nature, or because it is straightforward and necessary to communicate my takeaway. I might add a comment after the link (if space allows), such as in the following:

> Who Defines Women's Beauty http://bit.ly/tthm6t <- Aspiring to surround ourselves w/beauty is the natural order of things by @bizshrink

*continued from page 153*

"Finally, during those times when I simply want to click the retweet button and share what another has shared, I aspire to add a brief expression of support, as in:

Excellent! RT @mypromotion: Yay! Our crew won 'Class Champions' for the season at our #sailing club (BYC) tonight http://yfrog.com/h77sonkj"

# How to Use Private Messages on Twitter

Once you build your Twitter network and engage in conversations and RTs, you may want to share some private communication, known as "messages" on Twitter, or direct messages (DMs). Dawn Bugni is a master resume writer, certified professional resume writer, and owner of the Write Solution. She notes, "Once you find yourself with a direct link to people who can potentially affect your career, you may get excited. But stop a moment and think. You wouldn't walk up to a complete stranger and ask them to find a job for you, give you free coaching, or share complex advice. So don't do it on Twitter."

## DO'S AND DON'TS WHEN COMMUNICATING PRIVATELY ON TWITTER

These are Dawn's suggestions for moving conversations to private forums via Twitter:

Think about how you would interact in person and apply similar boundaries to online conversations. Focus on being generous and providing information before you ask for something.

Don't immediately DM your new connection with a request for help, information, guidance, job openings, sales leads, or career advice.

@JoeSmithCEODreamCo I'm looking for a job. I'm an engineer and want to work at your company. Can you send some links to open positions?

Instead, continue to build rapport by RTing him or her; occasionally add a personal note:

RT @JoeSmithCEODreamCo "10 new product rollouts for 2013" www .dreamcoblog.com <-- Excellent. Esp #5. Fascinating application.

continued from page 154

Usually RTing—sharing good information and sometimes personalizing it—encourages conversations.

However, don't use your RTs and @ mentions this way:

RT @JoeSmithCEODreamCo "10 new product rollouts for 2013" www .dreamcoblog.com <-- I've designed something like #5 before. Got a job for me?

Instead, ask a question or make a statement encouraging further dialogue; adding a compliment never hurts.

RT @JoeSmithCEODreamCo "10 prods for 2013" www.dreamcoblog.com <--Amazing tech. I must know more. *smile* Any plans for follow-up post?

@JoeSmithCEODreamCo Congratulations on 2013 product rollout. Great stuff! Followed your designs for years. Can't wait to see what's next!

Sometimes longer conversations naturally move to DM conversations, out of the public stream. It's perfectly appropriate to send a DM after several public exchanges:

@JoeSmithCEODreamCo (Didn't want to clutter the Twitter stream) As I was saying [continue your message].

Continue the conversations. @JoeSmithCEODreamCo will appreciate the consideration, and you've made it easier to send a DM the next time.

After there's been some type of public connection and a basic rapport has been established, most professionals don't mind helping others by offering quick bits of information or guidance. The most successful request asks for specific information and is respectful of professional boundaries and time limitations.

Don't ask for vague, general information or require the recipient to dig for information to help:

@JoeSmithCEODreamCo I want to work for your company. Take a look at my LinkedIn profile and let me know what you think.

@ JoeSmithCEODreamCo I need to make some industry connections. Can you give me a few names?

@JoeSmithCEODreamCo I want a job in your industry! Can you introduce me around?

Instead, after you've established reasonable rapport:

*continued from page 155*

> @JoeSmithCEODreamCo I'm a mech eng. Would you be willing to share insights into opps in your industry with me? Via 20-min phone convo or email Q&A?
>
> @JoeSmithCEODreamCo I've been studying _____ [specific technology or item pertinent to the reader] and found _____ info from xyz.com interesting. Any other recommendations for industry leaders?
>
> @JoeSmithCEODreamCo Congratulations on the Newsweek interview! Have questions about _____. Have a few minutes to discuss or point me in right direction?

Respectful, well-executed, and appropriately timed direct messages can lead to longer conversations in email exchanges, telephone calls, or face-to-face meetings. And, hopefully, eventually your next big opportunity. Remember, if someone is kind enough to offer additional guidance, by all means follow through. And don't forget to say thank you.

## BUILDING YOUR REPUTATION AND RELATIONSHIPS ON TWITTER

Hannah Morgan, recognized as one of Monster.com's 11 Job Search Bloggers to watch, provides advice and information related to job searching, reputation management, and social media strategies at CareerSherpa.net. These are her suggestions for enhancing your reputation by using Twitter:

There's a popular saying among Twitter fans: "Twitter isn't stupid if you follow smart people." If you follow people and brands on Twitter that add value or are somehow of interest, this tool can be quite helpful in building relationships.

What can you do to take your followers and those you follow to the next level? As with in-person networking, show interest in others and be genuine.

- **Reshare a tweet and add a sincere compliment:**
  Congrats @HeidiSiwak RT @ResumeStrategy: (applause, whistles, foot stomps) I taught her everything she knows (about Twitter and such)
- **Build onto a tweet by adding your own brief commentary/ reaction to the content:**
  So important! RT @YouTernMark: 20 Steps to Create, Expand, and Leverage Your Personal Brand http://bit.ly/w13zib

- **Promote others more than yourself:**
  RT @HeatherHuhman: Join my next free #jobseeker webinar on 11/30 at 2PM EST - http://ow.ly/7BGHm #JobAdvice #CareerAdvice
- **Help people who are seeking advice or information:**
  @Jobseeker re: oversees opportunities: ...have you looked at this site? http://bit.ly/tEo8wp
  Love Shally! RT @animal: Do U have a question for @Shally - he is my guest on Wed - send me questions about your sourcing problems
- **Respond to what your peeps are doing and saying:**
  Sounds amazing! RT @maryvandewiel: great crowd, gr8 energy + biz brand stories. nothing quite like seeing big talent step up @NY Brand Lab!
- **Take time on Friday (or any day of the week) to recognize someone for his or her talent, expertise, and knowledge via a #FF ("follow Friday") shout-out:**
  #FF #jobsearch gurus who rock: @Keppie_Careers @DawnRasmussen @JobHuntOrg @TimsStrategy @CareerDiva @phyllismufson @Absolutely_Abby
- **Thank people who have mentioned you (in bulk and sometimes individually):**
  Tx 4 RTs! @RandstadUSPros @TheJobQuest @jamesapolanco @instant-tech @vpiinc @lesechols @BlairAtVolt @SLO_OneStop @FandEcareers @writerdiehl @Careerbright @TheJobQuest Thanks so much for the RT ladies, have a splendid weekend!

## Overall Sharing Strategy

Chunk the tweets you send into quarters. By this I mean how you interact on Twitter: re-sharing, commenting, responding to questions and mentions, posing questions, promoting others, and giving thanks. Here's a framework to keep in mind as you interact on Twitter. This will help ensure your stream is interesting yet still on target:

25% Re-shared tweets from industry experts you admire.

25% News or events.

25% Your professional message and thank-you tweets.

25% Personal tweets to prove you are human.

Building relationships takes time. Don't expect to develop new best friends overnight. The secret to success on Twitter? Engage and be engaging!

# Career Success Steps

This chapter outlined many examples of how to tweet to connect with new contacts and expand your network. To be successful using Twitter, you must believe it has the potential to help you. From the examples in this chapter, you can see how a single tweet or reply can engage a key decision maker or influencer. It's not difficult to engage high-level contacts, even if you are a student or just starting out in your field.

Your to-do list is easy:

- Create a Twitter account.
- Write a targeted bio to help people find you.
- Find people to follow; engage with them by retweeting, sharing links to their blog posts, and asking them direct questions.
- Demonstrate your expertise. (See the lists of sample tweets as reminders of the different types of tweets you can send. For example, tweets with information or advice, tweets with links or news, and tweets showcasing your speaking engagements.)

While you can't expect immediate results, using Twitter offers the potential to create contacts who can change your career trajectory, introduce you to others who can help you, and further your career. There's no doubt Twitter offers a lot for job seekers. Don't miss any opportunities—dive in!

# 13 Communicating Professionally Using Facebook

**Y**ou may think Facebook is for playing games and sharing pictures of your vacations or children. However, according to research from Jobvite, a recruiting platform that delivers real-time recruiting intelligence with innovative technology for the social web, of the 78% of job seekers who attribute their job-search success to social networking, a whopping 18 million Americans credit Facebook for helping them land their current job. The data is not surprising when you consider the large number of Facebook users and the fact that most users have strong ties with their Facebook friends. These results are the natural outgrowth of the type of traditional networking career coaches have long recommended.

## Why Use Facebook?

It's easy to see how Facebook adheres to the reasons to use social media outlined in Chapter 10. You can:

- **Learn what thought leaders in your industry are thinking and writing about.** While Facebook traditionally is not an open network (where you can follow or track anyone you want without barriers), it has enabled ways to openly communicate and learn, even when you are not Facebook friends with your target. Some people set up "subscribe" buttons on their Facebook pages, allowing anyone to follow their public updates. Commenting may be limited, but it does provide access that was previously not available. Additionally, job seekers may choose to "like" pages set up by people to promote their professional interests.

  Many companies maintain a careers page on Facebook, and a subset of those organizations actively engage and interact with their potential hires on these sites. Most large companies, and many smaller businesses, use professional pages on Facebook to share information about their products and services. While accessibility varies depending on how engaged and responsive the company is, these company and career pages provide job seekers with instant access to interacting and learning what topics and conversations interest targeted organizations and recruiters.

- **Meet new people and expand your network.** In addition to using the tools mentioned here, you can expand your network on Facebook by engaging actively and creating public posts and a subscribe button for people who are not your immediate contacts.

  A variety of companies are investing in Facebook's power of connection by building professional applications to help you tap into a professional network (for example, BeKnown and BranchOut). We describe several in this chapter and provide suggestions for how to communicate well within these applications.

- **Demonstrate your expertise.** Most people think about Facebook as a purely social network and ignore the opportunity to network professionally with their friends. Don't miss the chance to let your network know about your career goals and interests.

- **Be found.** If you play your cards right, you can create a professional presence on Facebook and help people find you. There are a variety of tools to help people find you on Facebook (described in this chapter). Be sure to set your professional and contact information to be publicly available so it will be easier for people to find and contact you via Facebook.

Bottom line: ignore Facebook as a professional resource at your own peril! In this chapter, we'll illustrate how to communicate using this tool and what to say to help you get noticed.

## How to Set Up Your Facebook Profile

You're in luck. If you've read the previous social-media chapters, you have a head start to creating a complete, professional profile here. When you edit your profile, in the Work and Education section, add your work history, and describe your skills and accomplishments using keywords as you did in LinkedIn. Include your education and all your degrees. For the About You section, review your LinkedIn summary for inspiration. Be sure to pepper your work history with relevant industry and job keywords. (Review the LinkedIn chapter to recall how to select the right keywords for you.) Don't forget to include contact information—an email address and/or a personal website (a "social resume") will suffice. After you thoroughly fill out your Work and Education section and About You, you'll want to select "public" in the privacy settings. By doing so, recruiters and hiring managers who use Facebook to search for prospective candidates will be able to find you.

# How to Alert Your Network You Are Looking for a Job

Just as we wouldn't recommend walking up to someone you haven't seen in a while and saying, "Hey, I'm looking for a job. Can you help me?," we don't advise you to regularly use your Facebook status to directly ask for help with your job search. Instead, frequently share resources and information that relate to your target job to educate your community about your expertise. When you do this consistently, occasional updates about your job search will be more effective:

Here is a sample update letting contacts know your professional status without asking for anything (you can incorporate these updates frequently):

> So excited to be finishing up my culinary program at Johnson & Wales, looking forward to cooking up some great grub at a fine-dining establishment in Atlanta soon.

Use these types of updates liberally to gently alert and remind people about your professional expertise:

> Just read this article in Bon Appetit about the rise of French macaroons and what it means to the cupcake industry: [link].

> Researching [industry-publication name] to identify this year's trendiest ingredients. Surprised to find lemon—an old standby—high on the list. What are your favorite gourmet recipes including lemon? Here's mine: [link].

> I saw my favorite show, Top Chef, is casting in Atlanta this week. I'd love to be a contestant someday! Do you watch?

If you post these types of updates as your Facebook status, your community will know what you do and may think of you if they hear of opportunities. Every few weeks, consider posting a direct request as your status update:

As you may have noticed from my updates, I'm looking for a job as a chef at a fine-dining restaurant. If you know of anyone in an Atlanta restaurant, I'd love an introduction. Thanks for your help!

Thanks @FriendName for the wonderful introduction yesterday. I'm actively seeking an entry-level position or apprenticeship with an upscale restaurant in Atlanta. If you know anyone who works for [restaurant-group name], I'd be so grateful for an introduction.

## Is It Okay to Post Personal Updates?

We know what you're thinking: "Facebook is for personal updates. If I'm using it to let people know about my job hunt, can I still post about my vacations, my pets, or my significant other?" The answer is: "It depends." It's perfectly acceptable and expected to share personal details on Facebook. However, if you really want to demonstrate your professional goals and help your Facebook friends see you as someone they would be happy to recommend for a job opportunity, you need to keep that end goal in mind with every post. If you're complaining about your current boss (a definite no-no) or generally display a negative demeanor, most people would hesitate to put their reputations on the line to help you. Avoid highly charged, overly political, religious, and negative status updates. Feel free to share upbeat news as long as it would not prevent someone from recommending you for a job.

Appropriate personal update:

Really enjoyed our recent vacation to the Hamptons. It was great spending time with good friends.

Inappropriate personal update:

Really enjoyed our recent Hamptons trip. I wish I hadn't gotten so wasted on the last night. My idiot boss probably won't even notice I'm hungover.

# Create Designated
# Professional Space Inside Facebook

To supplement your updates on Facebook, you may also use third-party applications—platforms embedded into Facebook. These applications offer a way to create a "LinkedIn-like" professional-networking experience with your Facebook contacts. Two of the biggest and best known are BeKnown and BranchOut. These tools help you take advantage of the fact that your best networking contacts are more likely to be on Facebook than on any other social network. Both of these platforms allow you to segment your Facebook community into a targeted, professional group. (Be aware: you should still consider anything you post online to be public record.)

## BEKNOWN

BeKnown is a professional-networking application for Facebook created by Monster.com. (It is free. Search for it on Facebook, or go to beknown.com.) Charles Purdy is Monster's senior editor and resident career advice expert. He explains how job seekers can take advantage of BeKnown's professional applications and offers these tips on what to say:

### Inviting Contacts
BeKnown provides standard text to use when you invite someone to connect with you, but adding a personal note demonstrates thoughtfulness and professionalism, and can support why the connection makes sense (especially if you don't know the person well).

For instance:

> It was a pleasure meeting you at the _____ conference—I learned a lot from your presentation at the Third Tuesdays event. I'd like to add you to my professional network on BeKnown, so we can continue to stay in touch.

If you don't know the person at all, a compliment is a great ice breaker. Say you notice that a friend of a friend works in marketing at a company

*continued from page 164*

you might like to work at or do business with someday. You could pay a compliment to get the relationship started on the right foot. For instance:

> I loved your company's latest marketing campaign. I'm in marketing myself, at ABC Agency, and see that we've both worked with my former colleague Maggie Ames, so I wanted to introduce myself.

## Requesting Endorsements

Your BeKnown profile can include endorsements from people who can recommend you professionally. And with endorsements, it's important to consider quality, not just quantity. So ask for endorsements only from people who can truly recommend you on a professional level, and help them by providing a writing prompt. For instance:

> Hi, Juan. I wonder if you could provide a recommendation for me, via a BeKnown endorsement. I still have my 2007 performance review, in which you described my work as "outstanding" and praised my creative thinking—I'm very proud of that.

## Asking for Help

When you need to turn to your network for help—say you're starting a job search or trying to get new clients for your business—be careful not to send spam. Make your requests specific. Sending your entire network a note saying, "My interior-design firm is accepting new clients!" is not only annoying, it's also ineffective—because it does not speak directly to anyone, nor does it offer a tangible value. A better tactic is a targeted message to the right people. For instance:

> Hi, Rachel. I see that you have some connections at a regional hotel chain, and decorating midsize hotel lobbies is one of my areas of expertise. I'm on the hunt for new clients, and I wonder if we could discuss making an introduction.

## BRANCHOUT

BranchOut's community manager, Alison Hillman, oversees the professional network's social media and events, and Mike Del Ponte, marketing manager, focuses on brand strategy and public relations. They

*continued from page 165*

recommend the following three tips for job seekers who want to use BranchOut to land opportunities. (BranchOut is a free application. Search for it on Facebook, or visit branchout.com.)

**1. Search for inside connections, not just jobs.**

A BranchOut user in Florida recently found that the key to his job-search success was identifying whom he knew at the companies where he wanted to work.

First, he created a great profile with a professional picture, his work and educational history, specialties, and skills. One very clever way that he differentiated his profile from almost everyone else's was by focusing on results, not just responsibilities, when he described his work history. Here are some examples:

2009: Increased Market Share from 31.4% to 42.3%.
2010: Achieved National Ranking of #4 out of 470 sales reps.

Once he had a great profile, he made a list of 5 to 10 companies where he wanted to work. He searched for each company name on BranchOut, which illuminated the contacts he knew at those companies, including his friends and their connections on Facebook. Then he reached out to these contacts and asked for the names of hiring managers, industry-specific recruiters, and HR executives who were instrumental in the hiring process. He kept his messages short and to the point:

Hi Cindy,

I hope you're doing well. I saw on BranchOut that you are friends with John Thompson at ABC Company. John is recruiting to fill an enterprise sales position, which is very similar to the positions I've had in the past. Here are some of the results I've achieved in those positions:

- In 2009 I played a significant role increasing market share from 31.4% to 42.3%.
- In 2010 I achieved a national ranking of #4 out of 470 sales reps.
- In 2011 I closed 3 of my company's largest 5 deals, each over $1M.

Would you be kind enough to make an introduction to John on either BranchOut or via email? It would be a great help.

Thanks,

Tim

*continued from page 166*

Once Tim connected with the hiring managers and recruiters through introductions, he sent the following message and eventually got his resume in the hands of the decision makers at his target companies.

Dear John,

I'm happy Cindy connected us to discuss the enterprise sales position you are currently recruiting for. You can see my track record of growing revenues for every company I've worked for here [link to BranchOut profile]. These are three of the highlights:

- In 2009 I played a significant role increasing market share from 31.4% to 42.3%.
- In 2010 I achieved a national ranking of #4 out of 470 sales reps.
- In 2011 I closed 3 of my company's largest 5 deals, each over $1M.

I would love to have a short visit to explain some of my specific ideas to increase sales. Can you suggest a time that is convenient for you?

I'm looking forward to meeting soon. Cindy always sings your praises.

Best,

Tim

**2. Maintain your professional profile as if your next job depends on it (because it probably does).**

Posting a professional picture is an important way to communicate your professionalism. Ideally, you'll use headshots of you dressed in business or business-casual clothing, but don't be afraid to show off your personality and style in your photo, if it is appropriate for the job you want. In your BranchOut profile, you should also describe your skills, experiences, and areas of expertise in the Summary and Specialties section of your BranchOut profile. Here are some unique talking points that could differentiate you from other applicants:

- Travel:
  I've explored 12 countries on four continents.
  I've done three cross-country trips.
- Personal accomplishments:
  I've climbed Mount Kilimanjaro.
  I've run three marathons.

continued from page 167

- Volunteer work:
  I've donated my time weekly at Hope Women's Shelter for 2.5 years.
- Quirky skills:
  In college I memorized 10 Shakespeare sonnets and still know them all.
- Sports:
  I swam on the varsity swim team in college and swim laps three times a week.

When you're making your BranchOut profile, think about what your future employer wants. Usually this person wants someone who will get results from the business and will be a good fit for the company culture.

### 3. Stay on top of your friends' career activity.

Most people believe up to 80% of jobs are found through personal relationships and networking. If you engage in a dialogue about your career, pay attention to when friends are hiring, post when they are looking for a job, and keep up with trends, you will benefit professionally. BranchOut makes this process easy because its news feed and messaging platforms are designed specifically for career-related activities.

One BranchOut user, a woman in Atlanta, found her dream job the first day she used the application. She saw a relevant job post from a friend of a friend. She got an introduction from her friend and began a dialogue on BranchOut.

Her request for the introduction was simple:

Hi Julie, I saw on BranchOut that you are friends with Sarah, who posted a job that seems like a great fit for my skills and experiences. I would like to learn more about the position and potentially apply. An introduction from you would make a huge difference. Can you connect us via email or BranchOut? Thanks!

The next day, she met the woman who posted the job, a small-business owner located nearby. She was immediately offered the job and loves it! By monitoring the activity of the people in her network, she was easily able to find a great job opening and, more importantly, prove she could get an introduction to the person who posted a job, rather than having to apply "cold."

There are other tools to explore to benefit from professional connections on Facebook: Simply Hired, which has an application that allows you to actually see job openings at your friends' companies; GlassDoor.com's *Inside Connections*, which helps you identify contacts that could link you to jobs; and Jibe, which helps connect you via Facebook to people you already know who work at your target companies. (Remember when we suggested making your Work and Education and About You sections public? One reason is so you can take advantage of these tools.) To successfully access this data, your friends also need to allow their professional bios to be available to the public. That way, people you know can connect with you freely if a job opens at an organization where you have a contact.

## Professional Facebook "Pages"

If you are a job seeker who is also considering building a consulting or side business related to your target job while you are looking for work, one option for a professional presence on Facebook is to create a "page." Typically, businesses or personalities use pages to interact with their potential clients or customers. To create a page, visit https://www.facebook.com/pages/create.php. You'll probably select "public figure," unless you have a business to promote.

While we do not recommend it for all job seekers (you would not be able to access BeKnown, BranchOut, SimplyHired, or Glassdoor's *Inside Connections* with a page), having a professional page on Facebook may be a solution for people who are creating a strong professional community online. Professional pages are searchable on Google, and you can launch an advertising campaign to hire you via a business page (see the following for details about this option). If you find your growing network seems to spend most of their online time on Facebook, posting there (and pinging them with updates) could help cement your relationships.

Similar to a personal page, a professional page has various critical sections you'll want to be sure not to overlook: About, General

Information, Awards, and Contact Information. Fill out these sections as you have on your personal page. Feel free to post frequent updates on your page; take a cue from Rochelle Nation, a professional jewelry artist and instructor who sells her hand-forged jewelry creations online through her website, www.rochellenation.com, in galleries, and at art shows. She explains, "I prefer Facebook to other social-media platforms primarily due to ease of use for marketing. I can easily upload new pictures of my work, inform my customers of upcoming art shows, and share updates about new classes I am teaching. I also enjoy interacting with people on my Facebook page by responding to their comments relating to my posts. The monthly update telling the page owner how many new people 'liked' the page and how many people interacted with it is really helpful, too."

On her professional page's wall, Rochelle highlights awards, places she will be exhibiting, information about courses she's teaching, and her art:

> Guess who's been selected to join the 2012 Nunn Design Innovation Team? So very exciting, I can't wait to get started!

> Paideia Art Visions starts tomorrow! Support hand crafted art and stop by to see my work on display along with various other local artists. This Saturday (10am–5pm) and Sunday (12pm–5pm) [link]

> Interested in learning something new this month? Then check out my intro to beading and intro to resin classes at the Johns Creek Arts Center! Come make jewelry with me :)

> New Copper Cuffs! [with a picture]

## Paid Ad Campaign(s)

For a few dollars a day, Facebook can promote you to your target audience. First, you write a nifty ad stating you are looking for a position, and Facebook's paid ad campaign feature will post it to targeted members' pages based on geography, job title, and other targeting criteria.

According to Ian Greenleigh, a social media consultant who pens the blog "D2C—dare to comment," Facebook ads were key to his job-hunting success. When crafting his own ad, he decided to lead with the most "unique and appealing thing" about him in relation to social media—the nomination for the 2010 Texas Social Media Award. He goes on to say, "Everything else was straightforward. Tell people what you're looking for ('a job in social media') and include a call to action that gets them to click ('Can you help?'). Throw in a nice, professional picture of yourself, and you've got your ad." His ad follows:

**Headline:** *I want to work for you*

I'm Ian. I'm a nominee for the TX 2010 Social Media Award and I'm looking for a job in new media. Can you help?

**Other ads could lead with geography:**
**Headline:** *Compassionate Nurse seeks DC job*

I am a seasoned prenatal Nurse looking for a position in Metro DC. If you are thinking of hiring, let's get together and discuss it.

**Or they could specify a target company:**
**Headline:** *I want to work for Disney*

I'm Lauren. I recently received a BA in Human Resources and my dream is to work for Disney. Can you help?

As illustrated above, targeting is the key component to success with this type of approach. There are a plethora of job-search strategies to employ, so if you don't know yet the type of job you want, steer clear of this one. You'll get the best results when you can clearly articulate the profile of the person you're targeting (ages, education level, job type, etc.), so it's best to do your homework before you invest in this approach.

According to Ian, a paid campaign works. After putting together the list of key contacts and influencers he'd like to get his ad in front of, the total bill was just shy of $100 (for two years!). He admits he "would have spent triple on this, or more" for the results he's encountered.

Core to the success of your campaign is the zealousness with which you measure and tweak your ad, based on campaign statistics. Don't be too married to the copy; you may get better results by shaking it up every few days!

## What to Say to Attract Attention on Facebook

### *Be a Promoter*

According to Wikipedia, promoters "often build brands out of their own personalities and the parties they host. They may develop a loyal clientele that will follow them from one location to another." Facebook is a terrific platform for people who want to be promoters; they can host virtual "parties" and develop a local following.

We tapped Laurie Baggett, social media consultant to the medical community, to talk about her strategy for using Facebook. As a "natural promoter" of people, products, and services, Laurie has become a go-to resource for her Facebook friends and is a significant ally to her local businesses. Although articulating a specific strategy eluded her ("It's just authentic for me, so it's hard to outline a plan"), she did recognize that her intention is to help other people succeed.

This strategy landed Laurie a gig with Monarch Women's Wellness in Norfolk, Virginia. "I am constantly staying on top of what's out there—reading blogs and frequenting local, lesser-known establishments. I'm curious by nature; when I go into a place, I talk to people, I survey the environment, I become curious, and I parlay what I learn on Facebook. I'm always out there looking for the next great thing, person, company, product, or talent. If I find a great web programmer, I'll promote her, period, and not because I expect anything in return, but because I believe in her ability and want the world to know about her."

She continued: "Recently I shared internal marketing resources specific to the medical community—a passion of mine—and the owner of Monarch Women's Wellness found the resources valuable for her team, reached out to me, and, ultimately, hired me. My rule of thumb is: be useful. Invest in others, and they, naturally, will invest in you."

Here are 10 ways (inspired by Laurie Baggett's updates) to use your Facebook status update to promote people, products, and services so you can build your network, expand your reach, and be viewed as a go-to resource to your network.

Note: Remember, using the @ sign before a name or business creates a tag that appears on that person's or business's site.

1. **Recommend an event you attended.**
   Absolutely the best thing I've witnessed all year! SO glad I didn't miss out on this great event! Next time I'll be sure to participate.
2. **Endorse a favorite local establishment.** Start by making a list of every business you want to target. Business pages are run by other people, so when you like a page, it is almost as good as "liking" individual people. Targets could include:

- Your clients' businesses.
- Your business vendors.
- Your family's businesses.
- Your friends' businesses.
- Local businesses you frequent.

Identify and like pages associated with any person or organization you have on your target networking list. Keep in mind, if you create a business page on Facebook, these companies may choose to reciprocate and like your page!

> Love this place! Every woman needs a visit here! @TheFullCup-VirginiaBeach.

> Have you eaten at @TheGrill? If not, you are missing out! It's my go-to, favorite place for lunch or dinner.

### 3. Submit a recommendation to the event's (or establishment's) Facebook business page.

> Laurie Ramsey Baggett wrote a recommendation for Start Norfolk.

### 4. Share a job opening that isn't a fit for you.

> Don't miss out . . . and don't forget to submit your cover letter: Grow Interactive is looking for an interactive developer (front-end focus).

### 5. Give a shout-out to a new contact.

> So excited to finally have met Drew Ungvarsky of Grow Interactive! Yes, it's true. I'm a "stalker" of game changers, and Grow is one of those companies that creates brilliance and inspires me daily! Keep up the great work, Grow Interactive!

### 6. Congratulate a friend on a new venture.

> It's official! A new website: www.tiffanykrumins.com

### 7. Update your status during a live conference or event.

> Wow! Now that was a standing ovation for @SpeakerName—more than well deserved! C12 Keynote

### 8. Thank your mentor, boss, co-worker, or job-search buddy.

> @RachaelPierceJudy is the BEST investment I've ever made! I don't know what I'd do without her . . . She seriously rocks! I'm convinced there is no virtual assistant like her!

**9. Share a link relevant to your network.**

@LaurieRamseyBaggett recommends a link. Caesarean rate falls for first time in more than a decade, federal statistics show [link]

**10.   Announce a new local business or resource.**

There is a new marketing group in town and they just might change your business landscape and the world at the same time! Congratulations @asmallnation and to all the businesses who get to work with them! Brainchild of @SarahBray

## Ideas to Create Conversations

It could be a lot easier than you think to get people talking on Facebook. Lori Aitkenhead, owner of SocialCentric Marketing, suggests the following tactics to create conversations with members of your community and to call attention to your areas of expertise:

1. **Ask trivia questions and poll your friends.** Use open-ended questions to engage your community and get them talking. Post an opinion question, poll, or trivia to your wall. Here is an example of each:
   **Industry-related opinion questions (assume the poster is a dentist or in the dental field):** What is your opinion on whitening toothpastes? If you've used them, what was your experience?
   **Non-industry-related opinion questions (after the Super Bowl):** So, what was the most memorable Super Bowl commercial this year? We really like the Doritos commercial where the dog storms the boyfriend for a Dorito! So cute!
   **Trivia:** Post a picture of a celebrity's smile and ask people to guess who it belongs to. For example, many people would recognize smiles from Julia Roberts or Jack Nicholson.

2. **Use Google as a resource: Search a topic or current event and use the results to create Facebook posts.** Here are some examples:

Search: dentistry/teeth + World Series = articles about sports and dental injuries. A resulting post:

"Basketball and baseball are the two biggest mouth-injuring sports," reports Dr. Stephen Mitchell, of the University of Alabama's Department of Pediatric Dentistry. "And the most common injuries we see are broken, displaced or knocked-out teeth, and broken jaws." [link]

Search: dentistry/teeth + Halloween = articles about Halloween candy. Resulting post: Halloween Candy Buy-Back Program—Dentists have found a way to keep the fun, while helping kids and our troops deployed overseas. http://www.halloweencandybuyback.com/

3. **Tap into awareness days/weeks/months.** Make a connection between the current awareness week or month and something related to your industry. For example, November is Diabetes Awareness Month. Post:

"It's Diabetes Awareness Month! Did you know flossing can contribute to the prevention of diabetes? Flossing helps prevent gum disease, a condition that has the potential to affect your blood glucose control and thus contribute to the progression of diabetes. As if you needed another reason to floss, right?! Don't forget to do it after every meal!"

Additionally, there are always silly "awareness" topics each month that can get people talking just because they are so silly. For example, November 2 is National Deviled Egg Day. To make a connection, search "eggs and teeth health." Post:

Today is National Deviled Egg Day! Eggs are a great source of phosphorous, which is essential for healthy teeth! So, in observance of National Deviled Egg Day, here's our favorite recipe for Deviled Eggs! [link]

You might get people adding their own tips for making good deviled eggs. You may also encourage people to chat about silly awareness days/weeks/months. You never know what can spark a conversation.

## Be a Resource and Gain Trust

Sometimes you can build relationships and earn trust from networking contacts through Facebook simply by offering resources you believe would help them, even if they have nothing to do with your professional goals. Keith Privette is a business analyst for building or configuring and implementing emerging technologies. He explained his Facebook posting strategy: "Actually, these posts have very little to do with my day job. These posts help me connect with people in many different industries: H.R., marketing, public relations, technology, etc. The evidence I have that using Facebook this way works is that most of these posts generate real conversations with people I respect and value—people who share trusted relationships with me. This leads me to believe we build inherent trust with sharing our views over an article via Facebook."

No doubt, gaining trust is an important factor in job search. Consider using some of Keith's tactics on your Facebook page. Some sample posts:

Information for entrepreneurs:

6 Reasons to Build Your Start-up in a Coworking Space: The idea isn't new, but what you get for the money just keeps getting better. [link]

Do believe other cities are better poised to think this way & have the talent, communities, money to support long-term problem solving & innovation! Building for the Long Haul: TechCrunch [link]

Sharing a link to a potentially useful podcast:

I am listening to the 7DEESocialBiz Olivier Blanchard @thebrandbuilder (over 1,000 comments!) #BlogTalkRadio [link]

Commenting, and tagging someone else while starting a conversation:

Keith Privette via Kyle Coolbroth
Hey Zack Miller this is the model hampton roads needs to follow, more so than silicon valley! Kyle Coolbroth & Don Ball have truly transformed Minneapolis for startups of all shapes sizes and businesses. It takes government, colleges, universities, companies of all sizes and forward thinking people to make it happen. #Startnorfolk I do believe is a start to something big. When you are planning the next would love to be a part of the planning committee. I have a couple ideas...

Sharing information and calling out a city's accomplishments:

Google Chairman Schmidt lauds Minneapolis entrepreneurship—Minneapolis / St. Paul Business Journal

Sharing business-related news:

Salesforce.com Social-Media Tools to Challenge Likes of Jive—Businessweek: Salesforce.com Inc. is introducing software that helps customers create online marketing campaigns—and tightens ties between its social-media tools and flagship software, a development that may spur the company's own sales.

Posting information relevant to some of his community members and highlighting a contact's work:

Are you a parent with an autistic child or children? Are you a parent of a child with a learning disability? Are you an educator trying to find technology that can facilitate learning? Are you a parent teaching a young child to read? You need to check out this app! This app was inspired by Joey Hill and his wife that have two autistic boys. They stopped at nothing to getting this app made and promoting a new way of learning! Blood, Sweat, Tears, Heart, Love and Drive made this app a reality not only for their family but for a whole community just waiting for something like this to unlock learning for young children of all skill levels!

I have had the pleasure of meeting Joe and the team that made this app a reality. It is not your typical price point for an app, but every dollar spent will be returned 1000% when you crack the code of truly being able to communicate.

Sharing good news:

Aeir Talk: Just got the word, We have been Approved! App Store here we come!

Angela Smego is an insurance professional who uses her personal Facebook account to share useful links related to her field to enhance her personal brand—what people know about her professionally. She posts information about safe driving, watching for liability issues, and related topics. Her posts are useful for informing her network (for example, about recalls), but they also serve to remind her community about her expertise, should they need insurance information or coverage. Some of Angela's typical Facebook posts:

Distracted Driving Stems From More Than Cell Phone Use, Insurers Say [link] via @ijournal...According to insurers, cell phone use is not the only form of distraction leading to car accidents. A driver should never use a moving car as a mobile office, restaurant, or make up studio. Drive safely!

Follow up to Honda airbag recall story posted last month ... Air Bag Victim Lawyer Questions Honda Recall Scope [link]

Post-Irene Rebuilding Could Take Several More Months, N.Y. Group Says

This year's hurricane season was an unusually costly and damaging one for New York State residents.

Are you giving or receiving fine jewelry or art this holiday season? Don't forget to save your receipts or appraisals and call your account manager to schedule your valuable items on your insurance policy.

Another recall to report. If you own this car, follow the instructions from Ford and drive safely [link]

Some in Massachusetts Eye Tougher Cellphone Restrictions [link] via @cjournal

## If You Are Looking for Gigs

Many job seekers decide to hang a virtual shingle—they launch their own businesses in lieu of continuing to seek traditional work. Pamela Gottfried is a rabbi, parent, teacher, and author of *Found in Translation: Common Words of Uncommon Wisdom* (Lulu, 2010). She uses Facebook to inform her community about what she's writing, that she is available to speak (by sharing where she has spoken), and about her book. If you are thinking of launching a consulting business on the side, consider posting updates about projects you are working on and what has your attention. Use Pamela's updates to inspire you:

Shout-out to Carithers Flowers for making Found in Translation available in their Rosh Hashanah gift baskets, with guaranteed delivery before sundown! Happy New Year—L'shanah tovah!

Here is the first essay to emerge from my writer's notebook after the meeting of **Rabbis Without Borders** at the CLAL conference. Shabbat Shalom! [link]

Received warm welcome in Columbia, SC at Jewish Book Festival! Signed copies available there until Nov. 4th. [link]

## Company Pages

Companies vary in their response and interactivity on Facebook pages. Some companies set up pages but do not seem to monitor comments or reply to inquiries. However, if your target organization does maintain a lively Facebook presence, don't miss the chance to connect by visiting its sites and engaging with them. The organization is probably spending a lot of time, money, and effort to meet you on Facebook and will appreciate your efforts.

# Regular Business Pages

If a target company maintains an active page, visit frequently and comment often. Your best bet is to demonstrate your interest and passion for its brand, and don't hesitate to offer suggestions and advice related to your expertise.

Raj Singh is director of staffing at Intersil (www.intersil.com), an international company that designs and manufactures analog integrated circuits. He is also the co-founder of myJoblinx (www.facebook.com/myJoblinx), an application to help companies connect with job seekers via Facebook. Raj explains that at Intersil they have interviewed several people who contacted them first via Facebook.

This is Raj's advice for people who want to gain attention via a company's Facebook site:

If you're an active job seeker willing to publicly announce your search, Raj suggests that "before you apply for a position, go to the company's Facebook wall and engage with the company. You can say you are looking for a job. But be specific." For example:

> Hello! I am a _____, and I am very interested in the _____ position (req # 1234). Is it possible to speak to someone about this opportunity before I apply?

Raj explains, "By doing that, you distinguish yourself from the majority of people, who will just apply online and go into the database. If a recruiter is alerted about your interest, he or she can actually look for your application, instead of waiting for it to appear in a database search." He says, "Be sure to be specific with your post. Anyone who does this on the Intersil Facebook page will receive a reply from a recruiter."

If you are a passive job seeker and do not want to announce your intentions to find a new job, Raj suggests a more subtle approach. For example, comment on something posted on the company's page. He remembered one such commentator from a couple of years ago. The person responded to an announcement of a new part for a chip being produced for handheld displays. He said:

> This seems to be a pretty good solution for backlighting issues. Have you ever looked at part #_____ produced by _____. Note: the other part was built by a competitor.

Raj noted, "We were so intrigued that this person was so interested in a very detailed aspect of our work, recruiters looked him up and reached out to ask him to interview. While he was not hired, in other circumstances, he could have landed a job."

Other, hypothetical examples of how to communicate with a company on a regular business page:

If you want to work at Zappos, well known for its social media interaction and customer service, you may want to post (on your own page):

> Congratulations to @Zappos for their latest accomplishments and award for customer service: [link].

> I'm not surprised @Zappos is so well regarded. Congrats for making the list of great places to work [link].

Using @TheirName will post your note on their page as well as your own if you are connected to them via Facebook.

Consider focusing on something you can share that may interest Zappos, and post it on the company's wall:

> I've learned so much from reading about your customer service approach; my recent blog post is inspired by your successes: [link to blog].

> Studying customer responses and satisfaction based on wait time: [link to your research]

**When you post about Zappos on your wall, "tag" the company to ensure that someone there sees it:**

> Received a new pair of shoes from @Zappos today...LOVE them, and can't believe they got here in half the time promised! Thinking of buying a pair for my sister!

When you post on a company's wall, don't just say, "Love this" or "Great job." Avoid complaining, and try to think of ways to showcase your interest in the company.

## Careers Pages

David Cherry is senior business partner, EMEA talent acquisition, for McAfee, Inc., and co-creator of McAfee Careers' Facebook page. In *Social Networking for Career Success,* he tells job seekers, "Be interactive. Don't just visit a page and leave. 'Like' it. Leave comments, ask questions—actually engage with the company. Use the discussion forums to recommend suggestions about what you would like to see on the pages. The most common thing I try to encourage is feedback."

For example, a job seeker may post:

> I'm so glad to see your replies to questions here. I would love a link to opportunities internationally—particularly in _____. Thank you for your help.

> Wow—this site is great. Can you provide some details about how long we should expect to wait to hear about a position if we applied? How often is acceptable in terms of following up?

David explains, "As a user visiting our page, there isn't a set guideline about what we expect; the user should drive it, and we can then respond according their needs. Key advice: Don't be afraid to ask questions. It may be a corporate username, but we're real people at the other end, answering questions and writing the comments."

Sample, hypothetical questions:

I saw this post in Fortune Magazine about McAfee. Congratulations on this terrific press [link].

I was wondering if you could say something about how the recent acquisition of _____ company by _____ affects McAfee? Do you anticipate major changes?

## Career Success Steps

Create a great profile with a professional photo, work and educational history, specialties, and skills. Make sure you allow everyone to view these sections—do not keep them private. Differentiate your profile by focusing on results, not just responsibilities.

Stay abreast of the career activity in your network; keep up with trends to share; post a job that may interest the people in your community; engage in dialogue about their careers; and congratulate them on successes.

In addition to tapping into the larger Facebook platform for professional purposes, use third-party applications that enable interaction with folks in your professional network, such as:

- BeKnown (where you can create a professional profile and maintain professional contacts on Facebook, yet keep those activities separate from the more social activities that might be happening on your main profile).
- BranchOut (which offers a news feed and messaging platform designed specifically for career-related activities).

Consider creating a custom Facebook page to market a consulting arm or side business. Businesses use these pages to interact with potential clients and/or customers and, while it's not recommended for all job seekers, having a professional page on Facebook may be the solution for renaissance personalities or job seekers with a two-prong goal (a full-time job and a part-time business).

If a contact or potential mentor allows people to subscribe to their page, do so and keep up with their public posts.

Seek out the careers pages of your target companies. When you get to the page, "like" it, leave comments, ask questions, and engage with company representatives. Use the discussion forums to make suggestions about what you would like to see on the pages, and ask smart questions. Don't use these pages to ask if there are job openings; research opportunities and ask more in-depth questions about the organization or its needs.

Make a list of people, products, and services you want to promote. For example, implement this in your job search by: writing a recommendation on Facebook for retail organizations relevant to your industry; updating your status when you're attending an event or during a great speech; commenting on what others are doing; sharing job opportunities that may not be a good fit for you; promoting/recommending a blog/website that a contact writes/posts; and thanking someone publicly on Facebook.

Make a list of sources you can use to gather information to share with your network. Once you aggregate interesting items, you can: share a link to a potentially useful podcast; comment on, and tag someone else, to start a conversation; share information and call out a city's accomplishments; share business-related news; post information relevant for some of the community members and highlight a contact's work; and, of course, share good news.

# 14

# How to Communicate on Google+

G oogle+ is a relatively new, fast-growing social network. In some ways, it is similar to Facebook because it allows you to follow people's updates, write lengthy posts, and share links with your network. It also mimics Twitter; you do not need an introduction or permission to follow someone on this open network. Instead of "friends," like on Facebook, Google+ allows users to create "circles" of contacts. Circles are good for two reasons: they allow you to digest information from specific groups you select to follow, and then you can push selected content out to targeted audiences.

## How to Push Content to Targeted Audiences

If you are an optometrist, for instance, you may create circles (groups of contacts within Google+) of past clients. Once you establish a circle, you can post an update and designate it to go only to your selected audience. For example:

Don't forget to use your flexible spending money before year end! Call our office for an appointment today: 555-555-5555.

Did you see this article about how eating carrots can improve your eyesight? [link] Stay tuned for some recipes suitable for even the non-veggie lovers in your family!

A job seeker looking for a financial-planner role may create circles of other financial planners or people who share content about what is happening in the profession. Using Google+, he can easily follow what people in that circle post or provide content targeted to that group:

Have you seen the latest data on new home sales? Sales inching up—what does it mean for consumers? My take: [link]

Investing in bonds may not be a bad plan for younger clients. See what the Wall Street Journal is saying on page 1 today: [link]

You may allow your posts to be "public." In doing so, you use Google+ to broadcast your information to an exponential audience. Google indexes these posts and makes them accessible via search.

As illustrated, much like Twitter, Google+ can help you open doors to communicate with key contacts and influencers. The usefulness of Google+ depends on your industry and how many people you can locate who are actively using the network. Having a presence there, connecting with appropriate contacts, and making a point to communicate about your expertise via the network may make it easier for people to find you and see what you can offer professionally. There's no doubt this network has the potential to help you advance your goals.

- **Learn what thought leaders in your industry are thinking and writing about.** Once you identify people to include in your circles on Google+, it's easy to keep up with their posts.

- **Meet new people and expand your network.** The same principles apply here as apply to Twitter—there are no boundaries to connecting with people you do not know. You can communicate directly to people by using their Google+ name. For example, if you want to reach Miriam, you can use +MiriamSalpeter in your Google+ update. To reach Laura, +LauraLabovich.

- **Demonstrate your expertise.** Similar to LinkedIn and Twitter, Google+ allows you to demonstrate your expertise by posting updates. If you choose to make these messages public (which we recommend), you have an opportunity to reach exponential numbers of people. Your updates will be indexed and searchable on Google.

- **Be found.** Google uses various algorithms to determine how to tailor the results that come up when people search for a topic. (They call this "search plus your world.") The trend is to display results based on social search. This means that if Google can identify you as being connected (via Google+, for example) to the person searching, it is possible that your information (your blog, Twitter, LinkedIn, or Google+ posts) will appear as search results. How does this help you? One reason to use social networking is to be found. If you create an effective Google+ profile, contribute regular content, and interact professionally via Google+, it could help someone find you or something you've published.

    In addition, when you create public posts on Google+, Google will index them. In other words, creating content and sharing it is all you will need to do for a chance to be indexed and potentially found when someone else uses Google search to find information about what you know.

# Your Google+ Bio

First impressions count, and within Google+, that means your profile is king. Review and revise it until you clearly articulate your value to employers. While this is not a how-to guide to Google+, we'll cover key points to help you communicate your value and interact on this network.

## Introduction

Luckily, if you followed the instructions in the LinkedIn chapter, you can use something similar to your LinkedIn summary in this section. Target your audience, and incorporate keywords you want people to use when they are searching for you, which will "teach" Google search about your areas of expertise.

## Bragging Rights

Keep it professional here. It's tempting to add something funny or sarcastic, such as "survived raising teenage children" or "learned to avoid traffic in L.A." Instead, incorporate awards or professional accolades to help raise your reputation or credibility. For example:

Won Stevie Award for Sales & Marketing, 2012

Earned "Competitive Manuscript Award" from the American Accounting Association, 2012

Recognized as Manager of the Year, [organization name], 2012

## Occupation

You could simply include your job title here or add some flair or humor. For example:

- The Mad Scientist of Online Recruiting
- Resourceful marketing blogger . . . passionate about sharing ideas!
- Writer by day. Writer by night.

### *Employment*

Google+ uses your recent employment as your tagline; this information appears under your name and is the first thing people will see when they find you on Google+. Instead of just listing an employer name, expand the description of your current employment to include accolades or useful information:

Peachtree Petcare, Veterinarian caring for your pampered pup. American Veterinary Medical Foundation triple award winner.

Diamond International, Director of Human Resources, SPHR. President, SHRM of Oakland County. Creating HR processes from scratch.

Westfield Marriott, Banquet Manager. Creating unique, themed special occasions to meet all budgets.

Be sure to fill out this section completely, including all of your past jobs, as it can help employers who are searching for candidates decide if you are a qualified fit.

## How to Find People on Google+

There are a lot of different ways to identify people to follow on Google+.

**Use Google.** Go to Google and enter:
{site:plus.google.com google}.
Then include a keyword to help locate others in your field. For example:
{site:plus.google.com google nurse}.
Don't include the {    }s in your search.

- http://findpeopleonplus.com/: Indexes Google profiles. You can search by any keyword.
- http://www.gpeep.com/: You can register on this service to help other people find you.

- http://www.recommendedusers.com/: Suggests people in niche topics to circle.
- http://www.googleplussearchengine.com/: Use keywords to find people.

# What to Say on Google+

Luckily, learning what to say on Google+ isn't much different from learning what to say on Twitter or Facebook. While you have more space here to detail your opinions and expertise, you should use the same rules outlined in the Twitter and Facebook chapters to post on Google+.

## *Sample G+ Updates: Social Worker*

Dorlee M (+Dorlee M) is an MSW clinical social worker with an MBA (in marketing, from her former career). She uses Google+ to network, learn about new developments in the mental-health and career/leadership areas, and promote her social-work career-development blog, www.dorleem.com.

**Offering resources to followers:**

Great #psychology #mentalhealth sources: Some of these #twitter feeds you'll be familiar with, but some of them may be new to you... [links]

Important article on how the new normal is turbulence and how "we need to honour the past but we need to know how to learn from the future." #innovation #leadership [links]

Are you looking for good study guide tools to help you pass the #LMSW [link] exam?

**Providing advice from her expertise:**

To help you cultivate your capacity to keep on going:

**1.** Make sure your goals are utterly aligned with what's important to you
**2.** Be gentle with yourself
**3.** Be mindful... #resilience #worklife

**Linking to posts that followers might enjoy:**

The amazing power of #meditation...

## Sample G+ Updates: Fashion Coach

Ayo Fashola is a certified style coach™ and wardrobe consultant. She uses Google+ to build connections, foster relationships, and share resources relating to her background and experience as they relate to her target audiences. She highlights posts relevant to women entrepreneurs between the ages of 40 and 55 years old.

**Providing links to useful or fun resources:**

How to Dress 10lbs Slimmer!!! [link]

How To: Flirty Lashes and a Sexy Pout [link to demo video]

Do you shy away from wearing color? Does color SCARE you? Do you want to wear more color in fun, fresh ways, but are not quite sure where to begin? Here is something to get your color education moving in the right direction. This knowledge can be applied to how you dress.

**Offering inspirational advice:**

Becoming a woman full of confidence, beauty, grace, and charm comes from nurturing, cultivating, and developing your spiritual center. It comes from recognizing that you are one with life and life is one with you. It comes from recognizing that no matter how bad, or shameful, or guilty you feel about the past, every morning that you wake up is an opportunity to forgive yourself and start afresh. An opportunity to start anew and begin again.

**Expressing gratitude while reminding readers of her expertise:**

Highly looking forward to being in Dallas next week and getting into some closets. I feel so grateful to all my clients that believe in me and support me in my vision, path, and mission and most importantly allow me the JOY to play and express my passions in the best possible way. Thank you! Thank you! Thank you!

## Sample G+ Updates: Librarian

Luke Rosenberger (+LukeRosenberger) is director of library technology and historical collections at a health-science university library and is also a bilingual virtual reference librarian. He showcases his expertise:

**Providing links to useful resources:**

Don't miss this—you'll thank me. This is 5 minutes of pure awesome digital storytelling that my colleague +David Hale created for ignite dc #8, which was last night [link].

**Showcasing industry news:**

This is going to have enormous implications. Enormous. I'm encouraged by ACU's involvement in this, because of their very well-planned and well-researched "ACU Connected" effort that has been going since fall 2008 (http://www.acu.edu/technology/mobilelearning/). But this is going to affect the entire McAllen community in dramatic and unexpected ways. [link to students moving from ABCs to apps]

**Offering details about upcoming events:**

I'd encourage all my nearby colleagues interested in emerging technologies, education, and community outreach to consider an exciting new kind of professional development opportunity coming up at the end of this month. ActionCamp San Antonio is a chance for innovators from the local education and nonprofit communities to come together, share and learn from each other about strategies, technology tools, and experiences. ActionCamp uses the participatory "unconference" style to create an open environment for networking, discussion, live demos and lots of interaction. Anyone with something to contribute or with the desire to learn is welcomed and invited to join. ActionCamp San Antonio 2011 will be held Friday, October 28 from 9am – 4pm at the Courtyard San Antonio SeaWorld Westover Hills. Registration is only $25 for educators and nonprofits, and includes breakfast and lunch. For more details and registration, please go to http://conta .cc/actionsa2011. Kudos to +Molly Cox +Jeff Jackson +Colleen Pence +Debi Pfitzenmaier & +Fran Stephenson, who are doing such a great job pulling this event together!

**Sharing links to resources quoting him:**

I was a little nervous about being interviewed for this story, but I think it came out pretty well in the end. [link to Getting Schooled on Social Media, MySanAntonio.com]

## Letting People Know You Are Mentioning Them

If you use Facebook, you may be familiar with "tagging" someone in a post by putting the @ symbol before his or her name, thus alerting the person of the mention. Similarly, on Google+, you can tag someone in a post by adding + before a person's name. For example:

Just read +MiriamSalpeter's newest post. Have you thought about how to be generous online? [link]

Attended +LauraLabovich's job club. If you're in the Bethesda area, you don't want to miss the next meeting: [link]

### +1

Google+ encourages you to offer blog posts and Google+ updates your vote of confidence by clicking on the +1 button. This is another way to communicate online and to show appreciation. Don't hesitate to +1 anything you appreciate, but keep in mind that Google will index and may showcase your choices for others when they are searching online. Don't be casual when you offer a +1, and don't +1 anything you don't want everyone to know you read and liked.

## Other Ways to Communicate on Google+

Google+ is evolving, and the ways you'll be able to communicate and interact with potential colleagues, mentors, and new contacts will continue to change. You can use Hangouts (a video tool), Chats, and Games to touch base and expand your circle of friends. Keep in mind—whenever you are using an online tool, you have an opportunity to see or be seen by potential employers. (For example, some savvy recruiters search game forums to help identify potential hires for technology areas.) Communicate clearly, concisely, and with the intent to impress no matter where you spend time online.

## Career Success Steps

Go online with intent and purpose. Identify people with influence on Google+, and use the techniques suggested in this chapter and those in the Twitter chapter to communicate and connect with them.

- Create a Google+ account.
- Write a targeted profile to help people find you.
- Find people to follow; include people in your circles and interact with people you want to know by commenting on their posts and asking them direct questions.
- Demonstrate your expertise like the social worker, fashion consultant, and librarian profiled in this chapter.

As with any strategy, give it some time to work. It's possible you'll connect with a great contact in your first week using Google+, but it is more likely you will need to spend time lurking and reading and then posting and commenting many times before you connect with the perfect person. Remember, all it takes is one great contact to change your job search for the better; Google+ has the potential to introduce you to the one person you need to know.

CHAPTER

# Examples of How to Be Generous in Your Job Search

**Z**ig Ziglar—author and nationally renowned motivational speaker—has been known to say, "You can have everything you want in life if you just help enough other people get what they want." We couldn't agree more. Advocating giving-as-a-form-of-getting is not a new perspective or novel concept; in fact, it is just plain good karma—you do enough good things in this world, and the world is bound to listen.

Generosity means giving freely of yourself—your knowledge, expertise, time, or money—without expecting anything in return. Mastering generosity in the job search and truly expecting nothing in return is a challenge, particularly because the job-search process is all about YOU, isn't it? No. And since, according to Harvard Business School, 65%–85% of jobs are found through networking, a successful job search requires a team effort.

In Keith Ferazzi's best-selling book, *Never Eat Alone: And Other Secrets to Success, One Relationship at a Time* (Crown Business, 2005), Keith announces, "The time of the networking jerk is over," and stresses that we must "remember the number one key to success is generosity. Give your talents, give your contacts, and give your hard work to make others successful without keeping score."

## Communicating Generosity

Here are several ways you can apply the generosity principle to your career/job search, without keeping score:

1.  End every networking conversation with: *How can I help you?* Or: *If there is ever anything I can do for you, or your career, don't hesitate to ask me.* Don't fall prey to the belief that you are the only one reaping value from a conversation; consider that you too have something to offer your new contact. Seek to establish a long-term, mutually beneficial relationship, and you will find that you will quickly turn strangers into friends.

2.  Refer a friend or colleague to a position if you are not a fit.
    *Dear Tom, I really enjoyed our conversation today. Thank you so much for your time! I hope your meeting downtown today went well. I wanted to follow up to share the name of my colleague, [colleague name], with you, as he would be a stronger fit for the position that we discussed today. As you know, I'm looking to get off the road, but [colleague] enjoys the travel and also has consulting experience at Deloitte. I am certain he would add value from day one to your team. May I put you two in touch?*

3.  Send a relevant, timely, industry-specific article of interest to a colleague, mentor, hiring manager, or former colleague—just because.
    *Dear Louis, I was recently reading in the news about the program [Company X] is launching for sustainability. Not*

*sure if you've seen the article [attach link]. Thought it might be of interest to you, given your passion for the cause!*

4. Launch an unsolicited LinkedIn recommendation campaign, and find unique ways to endorse your most talented and trusted colleagues. This does not take a lot of time or effort, and it is a tremendous way to spread generosity throughout your network. Browse through your connections, or recall colleagues, supervisors, or peers who have had a profound impact on you, and create a thoughtful and unsolicited recommendation for them. Consider sending a message along these lines before you write your endorsement:

   *Dear Seth, I have been thinking back to the time in your department, under your tutelage, and I wanted to thank you somehow for the time you spent [showing me the ropes, mentoring me, guiding me, managing me, etc.], so I intend to give you a LinkedIn endorsement. Before I do that, I wanted to find out if there is anything in particular you'd like for it to say? I'd be happy to focus on anything that you are trying to accomplish in your career, so let me know if you have any specific requests.*

5. Offer to mentor a job seeker trying to break into a new field—a graduating college or high school student—or find ways to share knowledge with friends in new companies to help make the corporate culture feel less alienating.

   *Hello, Jonah! I wanted to let you know I was so impressed with your accomplishments and passion for IT. Please feel free to be in touch if you'd like to do some shadowing and spend some time with me at work. I'd like to do what I can to help you reach your goals.*

6. Follow the daily news feed on LinkedIn to stay abreast of promotions or job changes within your network; then send a personal, enthusiastic note congratulating a contact on his or her new venture.

*Dear Tina, I just noticed via LinkedIn that you have a new job at [Company X]; how exciting! I'd love to hear more about your new job when you get settled in. Just wanted to reach out and tell you how happy I am for you!*

7. Set up Google alerts during a job search for names of people you encounter while networking. This will keep you abreast of any happenings in your network. If a colleague, connection, or friend is quoted in the news or mentioned in a blog post, expeditiously respond with a congratulatory note.

   *Tamicka—Wow! I was so excited to read about your recent big win and mention in* U.S. News! *I am so thrilled for you and wishing you much continued success.*

8. Seek out ways to offer assistance, support, resources, ideas, etc.

   At the Career Cafe of Bethesda, Laura's Washington D.C.-based job club, a regular member arrives early each week in an effort to share announcements of local free and low-cost resources in the area for job seekers, small-business owners, and those looking for help with starting a business. It never fails: each week she does her homework and, as a result, at the end of the session her fellow job seekers seek her out to find out how she is so "in the know"!

9. Comb through your network. (If you are an active social-media user, it may be helpful to literally review your connections on LinkedIn, Twitter, Facebook, and Google+.) Find people who likely don't know each other and introduce them.

   *Dear Pat and Lisa,*
   *It was great to see each one of you in the past few weeks. I realized after my lunch with Lisa that the two of you would make great contacts for each other, since you*

*both work in pharmaceuticals! (I can't believe I haven't thought to put you in touch before now.) Here's a little information to get you started. I hope you'll plan to touch base soon. Otherwise, I will be sure to introduce you in person at our next big holiday get-together.*

### About Pat

*I've served on many volunteer committees with Pat and always admired her uncanny ability to get things done. As a territory/area sales manager at New Jersey Pharmaceuticals, she oversees new projects and strategic business initiatives and interacts with physicians on all levels. She has been especially successful in establishing contacts with chief medical information officers, and has won numerous awards for volume and new business in her current organization.*
*To top it all off, Pat's fun to work with and knows how to overcome any obstacle. She creates solutions to seemingly insurmountable concerns so everyone feels valued and as if their ideas are important.*
*Contact info: Pat@gmail.com, 123-555-1212*

### About Lisa

*Lisa is an industry specialist/sales representative for LR Pharmaceutical. We also know each other via a variety of volunteer organizations. I've been lucky to serve on committees with Lisa and applaud her leadership and communication style. At LRP, Lisa coordinates selling efforts and advises teams about marketing plans, with a focus on forecasting and measuring ROI. I know she'd love to take her expertise to the next level, and would be a great sales manager. (Since she's already doing the job!)*
*Lisa is also a laugh a minute; I've never spent time with her without leaving with a smile on my face. Even during*

*tense trustee meetings, she always manages to diffuse the situation.*

*Contact info: Lisa@gmail.com, 123-555-2121*

*I hope the two of you will plan to get together soon!*

10. Give praise and hearty thanks for the help you receive in the job search. If a friend writes you a glowing recommendation, offer to take him to dinner or coffee, or just send him a handwritten card from the heart.

## Generosity in Social Media

One fantastic outcome of social-networking sites such as Twitter and LinkedIn is the generosity these platforms inspire; this can occur on Twitter in the form of a "retweet" and on LinkedIn in the form of an "answer." Users realize the value of offering advice, sharing knowledge, and showcasing others' talents and are doing so generously and unselfishly.

### ⤷ CAREER SUCCESS TIP

Both online and offline, consider what's in it for the other person. The more generously you act without expecting anything in return (by suppressing your inner "networking jerk"), the more successful you will be, especially in your job search.

Networking, whether you are seeking a job or not, is always a give and take. You should be regularly keeping in touch, reaching out, exchanging information, sharing ideas, and trying to help an increasingly larger circle of colleagues and associates. It will come back to you in spades.

# Career Success Steps

- Make a list of contacts or colleagues who have helped you along your journey, in your career, or in your job search. This list can include friends, bosses, peers, networking acquaintances, fellow university alumni, and so on.
- End every networking conversation with "How can I help you?"
- Refer a friend or colleague to a position if you are not a fit.
- Send a relevant, timely, industry-specific article of interest to a colleague, mentor, hiring manager, or former colleague.
- Think about whom you can recommend on LinkedIn and write them recommendations.
- Offer to mentor a colleague or a job seeker.
- Follow the daily news feed on LinkedIn or set a Google alert to stay abreast of promotions or job changes within your network; then send a personal, enthusiastic note congratulating a contact on his or her new venture.
- Create a list of four pairs of people you'd like to introduce.
- Give praise and hearty thanks for the help you receive in the job search.

# Conclusion

As promised in our introduction, we've shared countless scripts and examples of what to say, and how to say it, during your job search. We hope you'll be inspired to return to the Career Success Steps sections at the end of each chapter to review and make a plan. Create a list of things you'd like to do first. Start with some things in your comfort zone—perhaps begin by introducing some friends to each other or writing recommendations on LinkedIn—and then move into more challenging territory, such as initiating a cold call or creating an engagement strategy for social media. You may find the most exciting opportunities await you as you push your usual limits. Remember, you never know where or when you will meet and impress the right person who will help lead you to your next opportunity. It is just as likely to be the man sitting next to you on an airplane as it is the woman whose information you retweet on Twitter or share via Facebook.

We're grateful to all of our colleagues who have generously shared their insights, expertise, and ideas with us! We want to continue the spirit of sharing and keeping in touch with you! Please visit our book's website, www.100ConversationsforCareerSuccess.com, for links to additional information, details about career experts featured in this book, and other advice to help your job search. Keep in touch (now you know how!), ask questions, and let us know how our book has helped you. We hope to hear from you soon!

To Your Success,
Laura and Miriam

# Contributors ▶

### Chapter 1
**Meg Guiseppi** is a C-level executive job-search coach with Executive Career Brand (www.executivecareerbrand.com). She is a seven-time certified career expert and author of *23 Ways You Sabotage Your Executive Job Search and How Your Brand Will Help You Land*.

**Barbara Safani**, owner of Career Solvers (www.careersolvers.com), is a quadruple-certified resume writer and six-time winner of the Toast of the Resume Writing Industry (TORI) competition. She is the author of two books on resume writing and job search and her work is featured in more than two dozen publications.

### Chapter 2
**Danielle Powers**, recruitment manager for MD Management Solutions, is a seasoned recruiter with extensive managerial training and sales. She is a 2009 recipient of RWN Up&Coming Business Woman Award.

**Katy Colvin**, P.H.R., has more than eight years of experience in H.R. working in various industries for companies such as Recall, PIC Group, and Marriott International. She is a senior H.R. business partner at Manhattan Associates, headquartered in Atlanta.

### Chapter 4

**Chris Havrilla** is a recruiter and consultant specializing in strategy, process, technology, and training projects pertaining to corporate recruiting, sourcing, H.R., and talent management. Companies retain her services via her company, Havrilla, LLC. Chris blogs at http://www.recruiterchicks.com.

**Mary Elizabeth Bradford** (www.maryelizabethbradford.com), known as the Career Artisan, is an author, speaker, resume writer, and award-winning job-search coach. Since 1995, she has been helping professionals worldwide focus on, find, and win their dream jobs.

### Chapter 6

**Kristin Johnson** is founder of Profession Direction, LLC (www .professiondirection.com). She is a multiple-certified career writer, social-media consultant, and coach with an approach that is cutting-edge, creative, and kind.

**Elizabeth Craig**, M.B.A., is a master career and job-search strategist at ELC Global (www.elcglobal.com), established in 1982. She assists stuck and frustrated young adults, mid-career professionals, and boomers in finding fulfilling opportunities.

**Joellyn Wittenstein Schwerdlin**, known as the Career Success Coach (www.career-success-coach.com), has been helping executives, managers, and professionals find their perfect career paths since 1991.

**Cali Williams Yost**, founder of Flex+Strategy Group/Work+Life Fit, Inc. (http://worklifefit.com/), is the author of *Work+Life: Finding the Fit That's Right for You* (Riverhead/Penguin Group, 2005). Cali also writes an award-winning blog and contributes to *Fast Company* blogs, where her work helps shape the global dialogue on work-and-life flexibility.

**Laura Gassner Otting** is the founder and president of the Nonprofit Professionals Advisory Group (www.nonprofitprofessionals.com), a national nonprofit executive-search firm that tailors retained search and leadership transition packages to its clients' various needs. She is the author of *Change Your Career: Transitioning to the Nonprofit Sector* (Kaplan Publishing, 2007).

**Laurie Berenson** is the president of Sterling Career Concepts, LLC (www.SterlingCareerConcepts.com). As a career strategist and certified resume writer, she works with clients on projects related to resume development, career change and transition, job-search strategy, interview coaching, and salary negotiation.

### Chapter 7

**Lynn Wong** is a senior manager in global logistics at a Fortune 500 company. She is a powerful community leader within organizations advocating globalization, education, and advancement for women and Asians.

### Chapter 9

**Debra Feldman** is the JobWhiz™ (jobwhiz.com), a nationally-recognized executive job search consultant who opens doors to the hidden job market for executives looking to expedite their corporate ascent.

**Jacqueline Whitmore** is the founder of the Protocol School of Palm Beach (http://etiquetteexpert.com), a premier business-etiquette consulting firm dedicated to helping executives polish their professionalism, enhance their interpersonal skills, and improve their personal brand. Jacqueline is the author of *Poised for Success* (St. Martin's Press, 2011) and *Business Class: Etiquette Essentials for Success at Work* (St. Martin's Press, 2005).

**Marci Alboher** is a vice president at Encore.org, a nonprofit think tank leading the call for encore careers—work with social impact in the second half of life. Marci is the author of *One Person—Multiple Careers* (Business Plus, 2007) and a sought-after authority on career and workplace trends.

**Farhana Rahman** is a global social-media manager for KIT Digital. Farhana also writes the popular blog Social Media Coolness (www. farhanastar.com), and she enthusiastically offers tips and tricks of the trade to her followers on Twitter.

**Mark Stelzner**, founder of Inflexion Advisors (www.inflexion advisors.com) and Job Angels (a grassroots nonprofit dedicated to helping people get back to work), is a noted thought leader in the human-resources community.

**Christine Comaford** (www.christinecomaford.com), *New York Times* best-selling author of *Rules for Renegades* (McGraw-Hill, 2007), helps CEOs in rapid-growth and turnaround scenarios achieve results.

### Chapter 11

**Susan Guarneri**, the Career Assessment Goddess (www.assessment goddess.com), a certified career counselor and career coach, is one of only nine Reach-certified master personal-branding strategists in the world. An early adopter of personal branding and online identity, she specializes in career focus, proactive job search, and branded communications.

**Jason Alba** is the author of *I'm on LinkedIn—Now What???* (Happy About, 2009) and founder of JibberJobber.com, a tool for job seekers, job hunters, recruiters, and headhunters to organize the job hunt and manage a professional network.

**Walter Akana**, founder of Threshold Consulting (www.threshold -consulting.com), is a career and life strategist who brings a unique blend of training and experience in coaching, personal branding, and online identity to guide mid-career clients who are hungry for change.

**Rabbi Karpov**, PhD (LinkedIn.com/in/RabbiRKarpov), has been writing resumes since her years as a technical writer. She was a Conservative pulpit rabbi (one of the first 10 women in the nation) and a teacher to Navajo Nation. She now focuses on resume writing and career coaching for executives.

**Kathy Bernard** is the author of the Get a Job! Tips blog (www.geta jobtips.com) and a career coach and workshop leader based in St. Louis, MO. She is also a "career doctor" on www.ilostmyjob.com, where she frequently leads free webinars.

**Bob McIntosh** (thingscareerrelated.wordpress.com) is a career trainer who leads and designs workshops at the Career Center of Lowell, MA. He has gained a reputation as the LinkedIn expert in and around the career center.

**Brenda Bernstein**, founder and senior editor of the Essay Expert, holds an English degree from Yale and a J.D. from N.Y.U. School of Law. She has been coaching professionals and students on their writing projects since 1999.

**Karen Siwak**, executive director and principal consultant with Resume Confidential (www.resumeconfidential.ca), is an award-winning, certified resume strategist specializing in helping people identify and articulate their unique brand and value proposition.

**Dorothy Tannahill-Moran** is a career-change agent with Next Chapter New Life (www.nextchapternewlife.com). She guides job seekers through career development, career change, and job search, and offers career tips and information at http://CareerMakeover ToolKitShouldIStayorShouldIGo.com/

## Chapter 12

**Rachel Sweeney** is a senior at Marist College majoring in fashion merchandising and minoring in business administration and product development. She twice interned with the top British brand Burberry.

**Hanna Phan** is a product manager at SlideRocket, a cloud-based presentation platform that brings ideas to life. Before joining Slide Rocket, she was a public-relations officer at Toastmasters District 21.

**Chuck Dietrich** is the C.E.O. of SlideRocket. He was most recently the general manager and vice president for Salesforce Mobile, which mobilizes Salesforce CRM, custom, and Force.com applications so that mobile professionals are always connected to their critical information.

**Jorgen Sundberg** is a social-media trainer and consultant specializing in LinkedIn, online branding, and recruitment. He is the founder and director of Link Humans, (http://linkhumans.com/), a social media consultancy based in London and Paris, and he blogs at http://jorgensundberg.net.

**Marian Schembari** is a blogger (http://marianlibrarian.com), traveler, and social-media thug who hails from Connecticut, lives in New Zealand, and works for a marketing agency. Marian has been featured in a variety of publications, including *Time* and *Real Simple*.

**Jacqui Barrett-Poindexter** is the chief career strategist for Career Trend (www.careertrend.com) and one of only 28 master resume writers (M.R.W.) globally. She composes career-positioning documents for forward-thinking professionals and executives.

**Dawn Bugni** is a master resume writer, certified professional resume writer, and owner of the Write Solution (www.write-solution.com).

A Twitter enthusiast and tell-it-like-it-is career professional, she is a former recruiter and has more than 25 years of corporate management experience.

**Hannah Morgan** (www.careersherpa.net) has been recognized as one of Monster.com's 11 Job Search Bloggers to watch. Experienced in helping displaced workers learn to search for their next opportunity, she provides advice and information related to job search, reputation management, and social-media strategies.

### Chapter 13

**Charles Purdy**, a senior member of the Monster marketing and P.R. team and author of *Urban Etiquette* (Council Oak Books, 2004), is a former managing editor of *MacWorld* magazine. Charles has appeared on CNN and Fox Business News, and his career advice has appeared in hundreds of publications, including *The Wall Street Journal* and Forbes.com.

**Alison Hillman**, community manager at BranchOut, oversees the professional network's social media and events. She previously worked as a community manager for Levi's, where she was a champion of emerging technologies.

**Mike DelPonte** is a marketing manager for BranchOut, where he oversees marketing, P.R., and brand strategy. Previously, he was the founder and C.E.O. of Sparkseed, a global nonprofit that invests in promising young social entrepreneurs.

**Laurie Baggett** (www.lauriebaggett.com) is a business-development specialist with expertise spearheading business relations, forging community partnerships, and launching start-ups with ease. As a self-professed "talent agent," Laurie's passion is "building the stage and shining the spotlight" and then watching her clients succeed.

**Lori Aitkenhead** is the director of marketing at SEO Bounty, a national S.E.O. and social-media marketing firm. Lori helps small-to medium-sized businesses execute their overall vision for growth by developing and implementing customized, strategic Internet marketing campaigns and services. Find Lori online at www.social-centricmarketing.com.

**Raj Singh** is co-founder of myJoblinx™ (www.myjoblinx.com), a tool to help you find a job using your network on Facebook. Raj is a global staffing director at Intersil who recruits professionals at all levels (interns to executives) around the world.

Thank you to the following people for sharing samples of their social-media updates or profiles with us:

**LinkedIn**
Traci Maddox
Richard Fuhr

**Twitter**
Ed Cabellon
Laura Schlafy
Stephanie True Moss

**Facebook**
Rochelle Nation
Keith Privette
Angela Smego
Rabbi Pamela Gottfried

**Google+**
DorleeM
Ayo Fashola
Luke Rosenberger